PRAISE FOR

Short Journey Home

"From math teacher to Buddhist Dharma teacher, fellow Quaker, Richard Brady's latest book, *Short Journey Home* is a lively and brilliantly written account of a life transformed. A work of imagination, generosity, and penetrating wisdom, guided over decades as a student of Zen Master Thich Nhat Hanh and the Plum Village community, Brady's is a life well lived, saturated with keen insight, character, and boundless heart."

— **VALERIE BROWN**, Buddhist-Quaker Dharma teacher in
the Plum Village tradition, author of *Hope Leans Forward* and
coauthor of *Healing Our Way Home*

"My life has been graced by spiritual teachers from a wide range of wisdom traditions. In this moving book, Richard Brady shares the story of how his life was blessed by his relationship with the great Vietnamese Buddhist teacher Thich Nhat Hanh. Richard's narrative is so vivid and vulnerable it left me feeling as if I had spent time with Thây himself. I highly recommend this book to people of any and all backgrounds who seek to make their own 'short journey home.' I think you'll find companionship here, as I did."

— **PARKER J. PALMER**, author of *Let Your Life Speak, A Hidden
Wholeness*, and *On the Brink of Everything*

"Every good student tries to follow their teacher's guidance, with varying degrees of success. In this very personal book, Richard Brady shows us, with humility and loving honesty, how he took on this formidable task. Through the inspiring teaching of Thich Nhat Hanh, enriched by Judaism and Quakerism, he finds ways to plant and water the seeds of awakening in the specific circumstances of his life. His stories are unique but will resound in all of us who have searched for the w

— **MIRABAI BUSH**
Other Home and (

"Embark on a transformative journey with Richard Brady's *Short Journey Home: Awakening to Freedom with Thich Nhat Hanh*, a compelling exploration of mindful living and self-discovery. Brady seamlessly weaves his life story with the profound teachings of Thich Nhat Hanh, guiding readers toward their own awakening through deepened connection with the present moment. Through vivid narratives and insightful reflections, the book offers a roadmap for navigating personal transformation and embracing an embodied spirituality. Brady's authenticity and the wisdom of Thầy converge in a powerful exploration of freedom. This evocative and transformative work invites readers to uncover their own stories, aspirations, and the path to their true selves—an engaging and timeless journey illuminated by the enduring teachings of Thich Nhat Hanh."

> —**MEENA SRINIVASAN**, Executive Director of Transformative Educational Leadership (TEL) and Author of *Teach, Breathe, Learn* and *SEL Every Day*

"Each story in this lovely collection is more than just a story. It is the discovery of a new insight, inviting us to awaken to our own insights on the path to freedom."

> —**DZUNG X. VO, MD**, *Author of The Mindful Teen: Powerful Skills to Help You Handle Stress One Moment at a Time*

"Richard Brady is both seeker and spiritual guide, one who deftly explores how Judaism, Quakerism, and his work with Thich Nat Hanh have illuminated his spirit and enabled profound transformation. His poignant narrative carries us compassionately through family drama and routine trauma, all the while expanding our understanding of his teacher and the Dharma. Brady demonstrates how and why the path is the way: The road is not always easy, but when this traveler walks it with his capacious heart, when he offers and receives the loving kindness forged in our myriad and dual roles as teachers and learners, the way home opens for author and reader alike."

> —**BRYAN K. GARMAN, PhD**, Head of School, Sidwell Friends School

SHORT JOURNEY HOME

Awakening to Freedom
with Thich Nhat Hanh

RICHARD BRADY

FOREWORD BY **KAIRA JEWEL LINGO**

Parallax Press
Berkeley, California

Published by
Parallax Press
P.O. Box 12327
Berkeley, California 94712

Parallax Press is the publishing division of Plum Village
Community of Engaged Buddhism
© 2024 Plum Village Community of Engaged Buddhism
All rights reserved

Cover art by KISYUU
Cover design by Katie Eberle
Interior design by Maureen Forys,
Happenstance Type-O-Rama

The stories in this book reflect the author's recollection of events.
Some names have been changed to protect the privacy of those depicted.
Dialogue has been re-created from memory.

Printed in Canada by Friesens
Printed on FSC certified paper

Library of Congress Cataloging-in-Publication Data available upon request

1 2 3 4 5 FRIESENS 29 28 27 26 25 24

To my parents
Jane and Rudy Brady

Wedding Day
PHOTO BY HANS BRADY

I have arrived. I am home. My destination is in each step.

—Thich Nhat Hanh

We shall not cease from exploration
And the end of all our exploring
Will be to arrive where we started
And know the place for the first time.
Through the unknown, remembered gate
When the last of earth left to discover
Is that which was the beginning;
At the source of the longest river
The voice of the hidden waterfall
And the children in the apple-tree
Not known, because not looked for
But heard, half-heard, in the stillness
Between two waves of the sea.

—T.S. Eliot, "Little Gidding," *Four Quartets*

CONTENTS

PART SIX: DOING AND BEING

EPILOGUE

FOREWORD

A memory that I will always treasure is when I visited Richard and his partner, Elisabeth, in their home in Vermont. One evening after dinner, Richard played for me the soulful folk music of Rabbi Shlomo Carlebach, one of the most influential composers and performers of Jewish religious music in the post–World War II era. In the quiet of the night, we listened deeply to the simple and innovative Hebrew love songs to the divine, full of spiritual longing and emotional depth. Richard was visibly moved as was I. I could see his ancestors shining through him, inviting me also to be fed by their beauty. The stories in this book are Richard's soul songs.

This is an extremely precious book that my dear friend, Richard Brady, has gifted us. I have practiced with him in the Plum Village community of Thich Nhat Hanh for nearly thirty years. Inspiring many others to walk the path of transformation and healing, he has been a dedicated student of our teacher and an energetic and committed cell in the larger body of this community. I have had the great fortune to learn from him, to receive wise counsel from him and Elisabeth, and to teach with him, co-leading retreats together for educators in Germany, Italy, the US, and beyond, both in person and online, spanning over a decade. What an honor to write the foreword to his sacred offering—an exquisite weaving of powerful personal stories, effective practices, and the gentle transmission of spiritual wisdom.

Richard's path, influenced by the richness and diversity of Jewish, Quaker, and Buddhist traditions, is a path with such heart, such transparency and vulnerability. Reading his memoir, we feel we are there with him as he discovers key truths about himself and about reality itself, whether it is in life-altering exchanges with Thich Nhat Hanh or senior monastics on retreats, in the loft of his home where he meditates daily, or among his community of fellow teachers and students at Sidwell Friends School, where he taught math and mindfulness for thirty-four years. Richard gives us an opportunity to intimately get to know Thich Nhat Hanh and his community through the eyes of one of his close disciples. As we journey with him, we are invited to immerse ourselves fully in the present moment—quietly walking alongside him through the forest paths of Plum Village and the busy school hallways, soaking in the wisdom of each step.

Richard is a profoundly gifted teacher who has been studying how to support transformation in himself and others for decades, and, with much life experience, he is quite effective at it. In these pages, you will find stories of healing intergenerational trauma, nurturing authentic relationships, and navigating depression with unwavering acceptance and compassion. This book gracefully communicates his hard-earned insight that nurturing wholesome qualities in our consciousness is just as important as taking care of our suffering. Richard's Dharma shines brightly, an irresistible blend of storyteller, wise elder, and playful youth, eyes sparkling with mischief.

Part poetry, part meditation manual, part memoir, this book is a doorway into what real spiritual evolution looks like. Through Richard's words, we are invited to traverse the landscapes of discipline, trust, and letting go—qualities that he embodies with grace and courage. His journey reflects a profound investigation into the causes and conditions that shape our consciousness and how we can begin to shift from habitual reactivity and denial to living with more and more presence, choice, and freedom. Through his vulnerability and deep love, Richard embodies the essence of true friendship—a friend not only to himself and his loved ones but also to his spiritual community and the world at large.

Richard's spiritual name, True Dharma Bridge, expresses his aspiration and vocation to serve as a guiding light on the path of awakening. In his presence, we find freedom—a freedom to embrace things just as they are and to learn from and celebrate the profound wisdom of a life well lived.

With deepest appreciation, reverence, and love,

KAIRA JEWEL LINGO

PROLOGUE

In *Short Journey Home*, I share my life story through the lens of the practice of mindful living that I learned from Thich Nhat Hanh. Through sharing events in my own path of practice, I hope to help you touch your own gifts and your own story.

What engenders meaningful change, and how does it affect body, mind, and spirit? I'll respond with more questions: What draws you to this book? Are you in the midst of waking up from an old dream, looking for a new story to replace one that no longer serves you? Do you need to share *your* aspirations and journey, *your* questions and struggles? However you respond, please read on. Together we can find a path home, a path to our true selves.

Thich Nhat Hanh was born in central Vietnam in 1926 and ordained as a monk at the age of sixteen. By the time he passed away at age ninety-five, in 2022, he had become one of the world's leading spiritual teachers. His students call him *Thầy*, the Vietnamese word for "teacher." *Nhat Hanh* means "one action." He always said the action to which his life was devoted was mindfulness. He also said that mindfulness must be engaged and throughout his books and talks, he emphasized that spiritual teaching must be *acted upon*, not just thought about, read, or discussed.

I was born in Chicago in 1944 and met Thich Nhat Hanh in 1987 when I was forty-three, first through his books and later at retreats and other practice gatherings in the US and France. The most important lesson I learned was the utmost importance of dwelling deeply in the present moment. I've come to call this *embodied spirituality*. To help others receive his teachings deeply, Thầy advised us not to take notes when he spoke. "If you do," he said, "you'll be receiving them at the level of the intellect, not as an energetic transmission." Transmission from heart to heart is the most enduring.

In the 1990s, as a way of returning home to himself, Thầy took up the practice of calligraphy, which he'd learned as a young monk. He began creating beautiful works of art using broad but delicate brush strokes. Each piece of calligraphy was a commentary on living mindfully. Here is one I love, simply the word *breathe*:

Other phrases he put into calligraphy were about dwelling in the here and now:

Present moment. Wonderful moment.

I have arrived. I am home.

Be free where you are.

Peace is every step.

Breathe, you are alive.

Breathe and smile.

You are enough.

This is it.

Some were about relationships and what he called *interbeing*:

You are life without boundaries.

A cloud never dies.

Peace in oneself, peace in the world.

The bread in your hand is the body of the cosmos.

Together we are one.

Happy teachers will change the world.

Go as a river.

I am in love with Mother Earth.

I am here for you.

To understand is to love.

We inter-are.

The way out is in.

No mud, no lotus.

The tears I shed yesterday have become rain.

And one that, to me, defied categorization:

Are you sure?

~

This is a book of stories—Thich Nhat Hanh's stories and stories from my own path of transformation. Stories are a way we humans have shared our thoughts and hearts for all the millennia we've been on the Earth.

Here is one from 2001 that frames all I learned from Thich Nhat Hanh.

Ted, my therapist, writes a few words on a pad, tears the sheet off, and says, "Here's your assignment, Richard." I look down. On the first line he's written *freedom from*, and halfway down the page I see the words *freedom to*. I suppress a sigh. *Will this really lead me somewhere?*

A few months earlier I'd received a message from Thich Nhat Hanh inviting me to receive lamp transmission to become a Dharma (the teachings of the Buddha) teacher in his tradition. The ceremony would be held just before Christmas in Plum Village, Thây's community in France. *I'm not a Dharma teacher,* I think. *I'm a math teacher.* I have begun bringing mindfulness into my high school classes to help students learn this life skill and increase their capacity to pay attention. I've also been leading mindfulness retreats for fellow educators. These are my ways of sharing the precious gifts I've received from Thây.

When I first heard this invitation might be coming, I began to worry about others' expectations. I don't want to travel around the country offering retreats and days of mindfulness like some Dharma teachers do. Perhaps I can call my friend Anh-Huong, who is Thây's niece, and ask her to discourage the invitation. But the invite arrives, and it's too late for anyone to intervene. I'm surely not worthy of this honor, but I defer to Thây's wisdom, trusting that this will help me grow. With that thought, I find myself deeply and humbly grateful.

During the ceremony, I'll be asked to present an "insight poem." I'm not a poet. I've written poems for Elisabeth on her birthdays and our anniversaries, but an *insight* poem presented at a formal ceremony before Thây and the Plum Village community? How on earth can I write that? My poem for Thây is supposed to express insight about something. Hmm. What might that be? Remembering the words of Marshall Rosenberg's nonviolent communication, I ask myself, "What's alive in me? What is my vision?" Since reading Thomas Wolfe in high school, I've been drawn to people who seem to be free: Henry Miller, Ram Dass, the Grateful Dead, Thich Nhat Hanh. I wish I had my own vision of freedom.

I've been reading alternative education texts and incorporating new methods into my math teaching, yet moments of true freedom in my personal life are rare. The weight of unresolved issues dating back to my childhood plagues my relationships, including with myself. I realize I'd like to learn something fresh about freedom that will inspire me. So I begin discussing it with friends. No insight appears. Finally, a month before the ceremony, I raise my questions with Ted: "What does freedom mean? Where have I found freedom in my life? Where should I be looking?" Twenty minutes into the session, Ted interrupts to ask how I am. Confused, I respond, "I've been telling you how I am for the last twenty minutes."

"No, you haven't," he says. "You've been telling me about your family, your school, and your spiritual community."

He asks a second time: "How are *you*?" I realize that I don't know. How am I? My habit is to look outside to find out how I am. Thoughts and feelings about others obscure my connection to myself and to my freedom. At the end of the session, Ted hands me the paper with the assignment. During the days that follow, I write responses for both categories: *freedom from* and *freedom to*. Nothing new shows up. Disappointed, I report my results to him at our next meeting. Taking in my disappointment, Ted listens, remaining present with me.

A few days later I wake up in the morning with a fresh understanding. I see that my knots—my habit energies—are a part of me and that untying them is *not* a prerequisite for freedom. This revelation manifests as a poem that I respectfully offer at my Dharma transmission ceremony a few weeks later:

> This freedom—not freedom *from*,
> from childhood habits,
> from childhood fears;
>
> not freedom *to*,
> to open to the love enfolding me,
> to know and live my truth.
>
> This freedom—freedom *with*,
> with habits, with fears,
> with heart protected,
> truth hidden deep inside.
>
> This freedom—freedom with this moment,
> just as it is.

RICHARD BRADY
True Dharma Bridge
Putney, Vermont
Spring 2023

PART ONE

TRANSFORMATION

In us are infinite varieties of seeds.
Some seeds are innate,
handed down by our ancestors.
Some were sown while we were still in the womb.
Others were sown when we were children.

The quality of our life
depends on the quality
of the seeds [that we water].
Practice conscious breathing
to water the seeds of awakening.

When sunlight shines,
it helps all vegetation grow.
When mindfulness shines,
it transforms all mental formations.

We recognize internal knots and latent tendencies
so we can transform them.
When our habit energies dissipate,
transformation at the base is there.

Transformation takes place
in our daily life.

To make the work of transformation easy,
practice with a Sangha.

When we realize that afflictions are no other than enlightenment,
we can ride the waves of birth and death in peace,
traveling in the boat of compassion on the ocean of delusion,
smiling the smile of non-fear.

THICH NHAT HANH,
Transformation at the
Base: Fifty Verses on the
Nature of Consciousness

~

Thich Nhat Hanh famously said, "This is like this, because that is like that," synthesizing the vast and complex teachings of Buddhism on causality. When we look at our life, if we see it as simply a progression of experiences, we miss the ways each moment is the result of multiple causes and conditions. To help us understand this, Thây often drew this diagram[1] as he lectured:

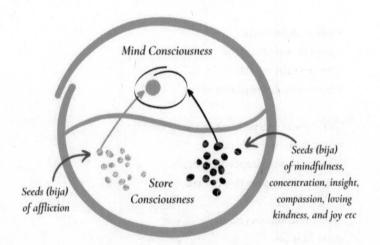

The circle represents the totality of consciousness.[1] "Mind consciousness" is the upper half, representing what we're aware of in the moment. "Store consciousness" is the lower half, the storehouse of all our potentialities—"seeds" of emotions, memories, tendencies, and so on. When a seed is watered by a thought, a sense impression, an intention, or an experience, it is likely to sprout into awareness. When it returns to store consciousness afterward, it is "stronger" for having had its moment in the sun. For example, while we're waiting at a red light or in a supermarket line, a seed of impatience might sprout. The next time we're in line, the likelihood of this seed sprouting is greater. But if waiting at the same red light, we water the seed of contemplation, then that seed will become stronger. Others can encourage our garden of consciousness, too, by watering our positive seeds. I often felt Thầy watering seeds in my store consciousness, encouraging me as I moved forward on the path of practice.

In November 2014, Thầy suffered a severe brain hemorrhage. A year later I had the opportunity to visit him in San Francisco where he'd come for various healing modalities following his stroke. As he sat in his wheelchair, I stood before him, bowed deeply, and gazed directly into his eyes. In Thầy's eyes, I saw his whole life, which I experienced as his unconditional offering to me. This was a transformational moment. It has stayed with me ever since. As I sat next to him at lunch that day, I was unable to focus on the nutritional food we were served, overwhelmed by the impulse to cry. I knew my life would never be the same.

Earlier that year I'd begun writing a memoir about my spiritual path and my life as an educator. It soon morphed into two books, one a guide for teaching mindfulness in the classroom,[2] the other, this account of Thầy's teachings, illustrated with stories about my emotional development and spiritual practice. This book has been the more difficult one to write. I had shared a few of these stories in intimate retreat settings but never before with those I didn't know well. To sustain the course of writing, I returned again and again to what Thầy had silently communicated to me that day in San

Francisco—through his eyes and through his whole being. As my seed of *bodhicitta* (Sanskrit for "mind of awakening" or as Thầy says, "the mind of love") continued to grow, I realized that the book I was writing should focus not only on my life events but also on the many ways Thầy's teachings transformed these events and, in fact, transformed my life itself.

Ultimately transformation is an inside job. But others can water seeds in us. Seeds that are watered grow and become better able to receive water in the future. When the sunlight of mindfulness brings other seeds into awareness, conditions are favorable for wisdom and compassion to grow.

We all have more or less the same seeds in our store consciousness. Through family history, genealogy, DNA, school, life experiences, and cultural reinforcement, some seeds grow stronger while others lose their power over us. When we become interested in our life path, Right Diligence, also called Right Effort, supports the practice of watering wholesome seeds.

The four practices associated with Right Diligence are (1) preventing unwholesome seeds that have not yet arisen from arising, (2) helping unwholesome seeds that have arisen return to storehouse consciousness, (3) watering the wholesome seeds in our store consciousness that have not yet arisen and asking our friends to do the same, and (4) nourishing the wholesome seeds that have already arisen so they will stay present in our mind consciousness and grow stronger.[3]

Thầy often shared the Buddha's teaching on the four categories of nutriments that we feed our body and mind: (1) edible foods, (2) sense impressions, (3) consciousness, and (4) volition, or intention.[4] By paying close attention to the "foods" we ingest and our body's responses, we can become aware of what serves us and what doesn't, what is healthy and what is toxic. Our volition helps determine whether our thoughts, words, and actions create happiness or suffering. Through the practice of mindfulness, we can observe the effects of these nutriments on our lives and make healthier choices, contributing to conditions that support wholesome transformation.

Chapter 1

WHO AM I?

If you look deeply into the palm of your hand, you will see
your parents and all generations of your ancestors. All of
them are alive in this moment. Each is present in your body.
You are the continuation of each of these people.

Thich Nhat Hanh,
Present Moment, Wonderful Moment

Spiritual Roots

When Thầy lights the lamp he's given me with the flame of his
own Dharma lamp, he is symbolically transmitting the authority
to teach a transmission handed down from teachers to students for
2,600 years, going back to Siddhārtha Gautama, the man we call the
Buddha ("Awakened One").

As for the "Richard" who received Thầy's flame, my origins, too,
are more than the newborn who came into this life in Chicago in
1944. I can trace my Jewish ancestry at least to the early 1800s in
Germany, my mother's family emigrating to the US in the late 1800s
and my father's in 1936. And my own journey in this lifetime is like a
stream with many tributaries feeding into it. During my early years in
Chicago, 1944 to 1952, these spiritual tributaries are mere trickles.

My family comes from the Reform Jewish tradition and observes no spiritual practices at home. The Reform movement arose in Germany in the nineteenth century as a liberal alternative to more formal sects. My younger brother, Bob, and I rarely go to synagogue, perhaps on the "High Holy Days" of Rosh Hashanah (Jewish new year) and Yom Kippur (day of atonement).

When I'm eight, we move to Glencoe, a suburban community on Chicago's North Shore, and Bob and I attend Sunday School at Lakeside Congregation for Reform Judaism. There we're taught an extreme version of the Reform tradition. There are no Hebrew lessons. Services are on Sundays, not Saturdays. What we learn at temple seems mostly intellectual. Neither the rabbi nor the teachers inspire me. We study Bible stories and suffer through interminable sermons. At home, we light Hanukkah candles in December. That's it! We don't observe any other practices or even talk about religion. My parents grew up in secular homes, so it makes sense. At the same time I see that even this minimal observance is important to my dad, and I wonder why. He seems to love taking us to the synagogue. Is it a way of instilling values in us, ones he has no words for? At home our family conversations focus on behavior, not meaning.

Two highlights of growing up in the Midwest are my dog and camp. I love Penny, our toy Boston bull terrier. Penny jumps on my bed, licks my face, and we snuggle for hours, extending into years. I spend four summers at Camp Nebagamon in northern Wisconsin where, for perhaps the first time, I live in the moment and discover what it's like to feel relaxed. Decades later during a bodywork session with my friend Elise, I'm transported back to one of our camp bonfires: I'm sitting quietly among campers and counselors around a huge pile of logs. Out of the darkness a flying ball of fire speeds down to the logs, setting them ablaze. As Elise gently holds her hand on my back, I again experience the magic of that night and others like it—fire, story, and song. I recognize my first spiritual stirrings, connections with an essence larger than myself.

Education

I'm a junior in high school, and Jim Landers, my English teacher, becomes my first mentor. He introduces me to American literature. New Trier High School in Winnetka, Illinois, requires all eleventh graders to write a junior theme, analyzing the works of an author who we select. Leaning on Mr. Landers' advice, I choose Thomas Wolfe. "Thomas Wolfe: A Theme" becomes the most important paper I will write in all my school years. For the first time, I've become interested in my own thinking. Immersed in Mr. Landers' encouragement and approval, I have a newfound feeling of self-worth, which infuses my writing.

In Wolfe's *Look Homeward Angel,* I read about a brother different from my own. Like Eugene Gant, I see that there's more to life than I find at home. I feel passion in the unfamiliar, a profound discovery for me, and I pour myself into my writing.

> *The main theme is suggested by the subtitle,* A Story of the Buried Life. *This has to do with man's eternal loneliness and inability to communicate with his fellow man. This idea is represented by "a stone, a leaf, an unfound door," objects of man's eternal search, and unspoken word with which he can communicate with other humans. It is Eugene's purpose to find these things. To do so he feels that he must escape from his "buried life" at home. The climax of the story comes in the last Chapter when Eugene talks to the ghost of his brother Ben.*
>
> *"Fool," said Ben, "what do you want to find?"*
>
> *"Myself, and an end to hunger, and the happy land," he answered. "For I believe in harbors at the end. O Ben, brother, and ghost, and stranger, you who could never speak, give me an answer now!"*

In Mr. Landers' class, I come alive, but it doesn't lead to meaningful conversations at home or anywhere else outside of class. As for Ben's final words, "There is no happy land. There is no end to hunger ... *You* are the world ... *this* is life," it's not until years later when I encounter teachings like Thich Nhat Hanh's *This is it!* and Jon Kabat-Zinn's *Wherever You Go, There You Are* that I am able to appreciate Wolfe's insight, bringing his protagonist back to the present moment.

My appreciation of depth continues in my senior English classes with Robert Boyle. His questions and comments are challenging, though, and I receive a C. My parents are sure it's unjustified, but I'm not. During the next semester, I slow down and reflect on my reading and my writing, becoming a better student of English—and of life.

I leave Chicago for Boston where I attend Massachusetts Institute of Technology, where I play a lot of bridge, learn math and physics, stop attending religious services altogether, and learn little about myself or life. The summer before my last year of college, I discover the magical realm of concerts, art films, poetry, and physical tenderness. Although my heart lacks the confidence to stay the course—these seeds have not been watered until now and are not ready to be exposed to the light—these doors of perception have been glimpsed.

In my senior year at MIT, I enroll in Huston Smith's class on world religions. I want to connect with religion, but I'm taken aback when he spends the whole first class recounting his LSD experiences. It's incomprehensible to me, and I drop the course.

I graduate in 1966. With the war in Vietnam raging, I apply to grad school to avoid the draft. I enroll at the University of Maryland where my California roommate introduces me to marijuana, catapulting me out of my everyday world, a great relief! A group of graduate students in physics forms a reading group; each of us contributes our favorite books to the office library. I discover in Ken Kesey's *One Flew over the Cuckoo's Nest* and Robert Heinlein's *Stranger in a Strange Land,* two outsider attempts to liberate those stuck inside the box. For the first time, I begin to ponder liberation. What role could it play in my life?

Russell, a friend in Chicago, tells me about Baba Ram Dass, a spiritual teacher who has just returned from India. I have no idea this is the same Jewish professor who turned on with Huston Smith. "I sat at his feet and absorbed everything he transmitted," says Russell. "I plan to get rid of all my possessions, go to India, and study with his teacher, Neem Karoli Baba. Ram Dass is speaking at Hunter College in New York next weekend. You've got to go!"

My seed of curiosity has grown stronger by now. Several house-mates and I drive to New York. The auditorium is packed but oddly still. The lights are low. We take some pills of unknown pedigree given to us by a friend. Ram Dass speaks in a quiet tone about fully encountering life, his presence even more powerful than his words. Every word, every moment speaks to me. Tears well up. He concludes by sounding a shofar, the ram's horn that I haven't heard since Yom Kippur services in Chicago, and I return from an altered state of consciousness. I have glimpsed life's mystery. A few weeks later I return to New York, this time to attend a Grateful Dead concert. My body and mind pulse with rhythm and rapture. Something inside me is being nourished.

Eight years after encountering the passionate writings of Thomas Wolfe, I discover a newfound intensity in the words of Henry Miller in *Tropic of Cancer* and his other books. I relish reading about his verve for life and his search for meaning. He waters important seeds in my store consciousness. Life is so much larger than I'd imagined.

Teacher

When I turn twenty-six, I'm no longer eligible for the draft, so I take leave from grad school to recharge my batteries. High school teaching appeals to me, and I land a job teaching mathematics at Woodrow Wilson High School in Northwest Washington, DC. Within days I know I have found my vocation. Saying goodbye to the world of elementary particles, I delight in the high energy of my students and the opportunity to help them learn and grow. I don't realize that I, too, am embarking on a new path of study and growth.

I remember my high school math well, but I need to learn how to teach. I begin by mimicking the way I've been taught: understand concepts and methods well enough to apply them in solving problems, then use them in subsequent learning. When I was a student, I found this approach effective and a source of pleasure. I'm not aware that there are other ways of teaching mathematics. My success as a high school student gives me false confidence in this approach.

Fortunately I have to take several education courses. That summer I enroll in a class called Methods and Principles of Secondary Education. I've heard that education courses are generally a waste of time, so I hope to get away with infrequent attendance. In the first class, the professor seems to be on autopilot. Teachers needing continuing education units (CEU's) overflow the room. When the professor tells us a second section will be offered, I sign up for that one. Anything has to be better than this.

At the beginning of his first class, Ron McKeen, the overflow instructor, holds up our textbook and says, astonishingly, "We won't be using this." Instead he reads us a newspaper op-ed on the new constitutional amendment granting eighteen-year-olds the right to vote. This turns out to be his approach, introducing a think piece, then inviting discussion. The course becomes a collaboration between Ron and us, his students. Near the end of the summer semester, we divide into groups to design projects we'll present to the whole class.

Inspired by a music teacher in our small group, we experiment with the Orff-Schulwerk method of spontaneous experimentation to teach music making. Sitting in a large circle on the floor and holding percussion instruments, we listen, respond, and improvise. One class member establishes a beat which the rest of us pick up. Soon new strands are weaving in and out, sounds rising and falling. I feel a sense of connection and transiency. In this rich classroom environment, there are no papers, tests, quizzes, or exams. We draw our semester grades from a hat—all A's. It's a totally new, mind-boggling way for me to understand education. Inspired by Ron's class, I begin poring over books on alternative education, making my way from Postman and Weingartner's *Teaching as a Subversive Activity* to A.S. Neill's *Summerhill* and Paolo Freire's *Pedagogy of the Oppressed*.

Throughout the term, we're asked "What does education mean?" We share joy, anger, humor, and frustration, an environment that brings out everyone's creativity. We ask questions, challenge so-called truths, play with ideas, try out new roles, create philosophies, joke, take risks, and analyze what's happening each step of the way. Everything evolves from this process and is incorporated into it. I've never known inspiration to flow so easily with only a few prompts.

This summer I also have an opportunity to attend a math class for elementary school teachers taught by a friend of Ron's named Neil Davidson. There I see teachers sitting in small groups excitedly proving a property of parallelograms. This is a *boldly* new way of learning mathematics, from the inside out! For me, it's a game-changer.

Chapter 2

REVELATION

The now is the only moment when and where you can find what you have been looking for. You have been searching for Nirvana. You have been looking for God. You have been looking for enlightenment, for awakening. You have been looking for the Pure Land, and for your true nature of no birth and no death. It turns out that everything you have been looking for is already there in the present moment. And the secret of the finding is to go back to the now.

Thich Nhat Hanh,
Inside the Now: Meditations on Time

The Quaker Stream

Two years after Ron opened my understanding of teaching, I'm available to receive lessons in spirituality, although I don't quite realize it. When I begin teaching at Sidwell Friends, a pre-K through high school in Washington, DC, and Bethesda, MD, I've never even heard the word *mystic*. However, at twenty-nine, I'm surprised to find how meaningful the weekly upper school Meeting for Worship becomes. I cherish sitting in the silent gymnasium for forty minutes each Thursday morning, surrounded by students and faculty. There are moments my heart starts to pound. Something is stirring inside. Responding to it without thinking, I rise to my feet and speak what comes from within as is the custom in a Quaker meeting. Occasionally, a message comes without the impulse to stand, I just sit with the "message." Sometimes it goes away. If it continues to draw my attention, I sense it's to be shared.

Later in life when I sit in silent Buddhist meditation, not once does my body tell me to rise and offer vocal ministry. Those settings don't invite it. In Quaker worship, however, they do. In these initial experiences of listening in the silence of worship, I welcome my inner openings. A part of me that has been asleep feels awakened. I am at home and encouraged by a newly discovered light inside me. I feel connected to the students and other faculty members sitting with me in this stillness.

Reflection and Contemplation

I embrace the silence of Quaker worship quite naturally. As a youngster, I took refuge in the solitude of my bedroom, sometimes with my dog Penny, often alone. Lying on my bed, I reflected on life—usually mine—sorting out and re-sorting the past, planning and replanning the future. I rarely enjoyed the present moment.

Reflection took on a new shape in high school where challenging geometry problems became objects of reflection. It was usually productive, but sometimes I'd think over the properties of a geometric figure and discover no way to proceed. On those occasions, I stopped thinking and just gazed at the figure, my mind open to whatever it might tell me. The figure had become an object of contemplation. *Doing* had given way to *being with*.

Sitting in Quaker worship has similarities. If I don't enter the gym mulling over a problem or a decision facing me, one often comes to mind soon after I sit down. Following some reflection, a resolution may arise. Sometimes resolution comes out of nowhere—a total surprise. Sometimes I short-circuit my thinking mind and wait for a resolution to arise from a deeper place. Quakers call this contemplative *being with* "holding in the Light," a turning over to the Spirit.

Hawaii

In 1975, during spring break of my second year at Sidwell Friends School, Mom, Dad, Bob, and I take a vacation to Maui. I find the setting glorious, the weather relaxing, and the entire experience a welcome respite from teaching. We enjoy driving around the island, swimming, and basking in the tropical sun. As our time on Maui draws to a close, Bob eats something that irritates his fragile digestive system. He starts to bleed internally and is rushed to the small island hospital where he receives blood transfusions. By evening, we're informed that the hospital has exhausted its supply of plasma. A fresh supply is due from Oahu on the first plane in the morning. While Mom and Dad sit with Bob in his room, I wait outside in the hall trying in vain to read. I want to allow my parents their own time with Bob and hope to have my time later. Late in the night my parents emerge from Bob's room, emotionally and physically exhausted. I say good night to them, then open the door and go in. Bob is resting quietly on his bed in the darkened room. *Will he live through the night? How can I fully be with him in this moment?*

I've never talked with Bob about spiritual matters or anything else of consequence. As I speak to him now, I center myself and settle into a state of worship. I share with him my experience of Quaker worship. Everything outside the present moment falls away, and I feel an energy in the room, something I've only felt a few times before. I feel deeply connected with him and sense that we are being held by something larger. After I finish talking, we sit in silence. I doze off several times. At sunrise Bob is still holding on. Mom and

Dad join us. Shortly afterward, the fresh plasma arrives. I'm grateful, awestruck.

Meeting for worship has become an important part of my life, and I jump at the chance to participate in a faculty study group with our headmaster, Bob Smith. We read English Quaker George Gorman's Swarthmore lecture *The Amazing Fact of Quaker Worship*. Bob is one of the few Quakers on the staff. No one has spoken to me about meeting for worship, yet I find Gorman's small book totally familiar for some reason I can't fathom.

I'm saddened when student misbehavior leads our upper school faculty to suspend our all-school meeting. In its place we have several smaller, biweekly Meetings for Worship. These alternate with small "Centered Meetings" on topics proposed and hosted by faculty members and a few students. I decide to offer a Centered Meeting using the Smithsonian's jazz recordings. I love jazz and want to share my passion with students. I also hope our shared listening will support Meeting for Worship. I'm taken aback when I find that a number of the students who chose this group are not able to focus on listening. They fiddle or find some distraction. Had I known then about meditation, I might have begun each session with a mindfulness exercise.

After a couple of frustrating semesters of jazz, I shift to offering a Centered Meeting on Martin Buber. I've recently read Buber's *The Way of Response* and am eager to share his teachings. Two students take home copies and select passages to share out of the silence at our next meeting. As in Meeting for Worship, other students are free to respond out of the silence that ensues. Buber is more engaging for students, but the depth of his thinking is sometimes over all our heads.

Listening to Irish music, hosted by two seniors, becomes a welcome change. I have no special responsibility and can just settle into the music, which I discover expresses the full gamut of human emotion. I begin to wonder what it's like to attend a Meeting for Worship where participants are there by choice and attendees are actually Quaker. During school vacation, I attend Bethesda Friends Meeting, which meets at Sidwell Friends Lower School. At the close of worship, guests introduce themselves and say a few words. I rise and say I've looked forward to worshiping with Quakers and am surprised by my disappointment. Although most upper school students and faculty are not of the Quaker faith, they are my community. I miss their familiar faces and voices. For the first time I appreciate the importance of spiritual community. I don't go on to say what a gift it is to be able to worship with 400 young people, many of them searching for answers to questions about themselves and their world, some willing to share their inner inquiry in meeting. In this day's messages, no one has been the least bit vulnerable, or so it seems to me, and I miss that.

Pendle Hill

After ten years at Sidwell, I'm eligible for a sabbatical. I enroll in Buffalo State College's Creative Studies master's program for the 1983 fall term and at Pendle Hill, a Quaker study and retreat center, for the winter. At Pendle Hill, I hope to have time to reflect on what I've discovered about teaching, learn more about Quakerism, and perhaps do some writing. I plan to conclude my sabbatical by traveling around the country visiting schools with innovative math programs.

Meeting for Worship is at the heart of the Pendle Hill experience. Arriving in early January 1984, I find the meeting room vibrant with energy from decades of deeply held worship. Each day after breakfast we have a half-hour Meeting for Worship. I find it easy to slip into a warm, attuned state. From the stillness, questions and answers arise. Most of my thirty-five fellow students are my age or older, many facing life transitions—retirement, death of a spouse, divorce, loss of a job. At age thirty-nine, what am I doing here? It's clear that I haven't come *just* to learn about Quakerism but to search my soul.

By the end of the second week, I realize I need to stay on through the spring term. Something is percolating inside me.

I'm assigned Parker Palmer as my consultant. We meet weekly for a conversation about life—going for a walk, weather permitting. I discover that Parker graduated from my high school four years before me. Perhaps this accounts for his sense of humor. In my initial term, I enroll in Parker's course Tales of the Journey, my first experience of spiritual education. He is an author, educator, and activist who focuses on education, community, leadership, spirituality, and social change. I've recently read his new book, *To Know As We Are Known: A Spirituality of Education.* The pedagogy he describes bears a close resemblance to that I used in my Martin Buber Centered Meeting and what I later found in Quaker worship sharing and still later in Buddhist Dharma sharing. Each provides a spiritual container where participants can share their suffering and joy. At the end of every class, Parker gives us an aphorism related to journeys and invites us to journal on it in the coming week. In response to a prompt from Dante, "In the middle of the journey of our life, / I found myself within a dark woods / where the straight way was lost," I write:

> *Listening to jazz improvisation, I sometimes lose the thread of the tune as musicians enter the zone that makes the piece unique to them at the moment. Written by others, the tune is the improvisor's point of departure, also its resolution. While I'm lost, they are not. The improvisors wander off the straight way to create their own detour, their own exploration.*

> *The straight way is the way of my father. Generations have followed this path, glancing up from time to time for reassuring looks at the road signs lettered by various hands—road signs that read, "Father Went This Way."*

> *The straight way is abandoned, but I am not. I have discovered a detour that brings forth the artistry and talent bequeathed to me*

by my mother. My life has become a jazz improv. Exciting! Oh,
but I need some guidance.

I find some in my second winter course, Bill Taber's Quaker
Journals. Quaker journals leave a personal record of the role God
has played in the authors' lives as a testimony for those who follow.
Our class visits Pendle Hill's extensive collection of Quaker journals
dating back to the beginning of the religion in the 1660s. Each of
us selects two journals to read, one written during Quakerism's first
150 years, the other written later. Each week, two of us offer presentations on what we've read.

The earlier journal I choose was written by Sarah Grubb, an
English Quaker who lived from 1756 to 1790. I'm drawn to her in
part because she's a teacher. As I read her journal, I copy passages
like this one onto three-by-five cards:

> *As to the performance of great works, I look not for it; my mind*
> *is taught to believe that I have no right thereto, or reason to*
> *expect that an instrument so feeble as myself, and so little a time*
> *in use, is likely to be owned, in any extraordinary degree, in the*
> *discharge of my small part of the great work. But my spirit hath*
> *often been dipped into sympathy inexpressible, with a seed in*
> *those parts, of which I have not yet attained outward discovery.*[5]

I might have written these words myself, about my hope to make
changes in the conservative culture of Sidwell Friends. Although
Sarah Grubb lived and wrote three hundred years before me, she's
familiar. I have a sudden epiphany. She and I are the same Myers-
Briggs personality type, INTJ (introverted, intuitive, thinking, judging). The Myers- Briggs Type Indicator, based on the work of C. G.
Jung, describes INTJ individuals as "independent, strategic, logical,
reserved, insightful, and driven by their own original ideas to achieve
improvements."[6] Sarah and I experience life in a similar way. I delay
my presentation a week so I can spend more time with the journal of
this newfound sister and deepen my understanding of her.

Sarah is a person of deep faith in God who subjugates her own will to guidance from Spirit. While Sarah thus received instructions for her life, the thought that my own inner guide might be grounded in Spirit never even crosses my mind. My connection to Spirit is still young and undeveloped. I'm routinely directed by will, not obedience. Nor am I ready for Sarah's level of commitment to the spiritual life.

Judaism Revisited

At Sidwell Friends and Pendle Hill, I learn more about Quakerism than I've ever known about Judaism. Later, during the 1990s, I learn even more about Buddhism. My ancestors transmitted their traits and passed on their Judaism, but when I left home, I didn't take their Judaism with me. At Pendle Hill, I find a resonance with Polish-born American Rabbi Abraham Joshua Heschel through his book *A Passion for Truth*, which leads me to reflect on the absence of religious instruction in my youth. Why didn't my father talk about Judaism? Parker suggests that the previous generation wasn't in the habit of sharing their faith out loud and recommends that I attend services at the Jewish Renewal Congregation B'nai Or in the Germantown section of Philadelphia. Jewish Renewal is a burgeoning movement founded around the teachings of Reb Zalman Schachter-Shalomi to reinvigorate modern Judaism with tradition, mysticism, and music.

On a beautiful spring morning I find a large white frame house, the porch spilling over with adults and children. Much of the service is in Hebrew, which I don't understand, but the chanting, singing, dancing, and joy make me feel I've come home to the spiritual community I never had. Dormant Jewish seeds in me are being watered. If I could just find a group like this in Washington, I would learn Hebrew. But when I return to Washington, I learn there is no Jewish Renewal congregation there.

On a visit to my parents two years later, in 1986, my fiancée Elisabeth and I attend temple with my father for the first time in my adult life. His singing of the prayers is so beautiful I'm moved to tears. Later in the visit I ask about his Judaism. When he confirms my understanding that his parents weren't observant, I inquire, "Still, it seems Judaism is important to you. Am I right?"

"Yes, you're right," he says.

"Why?" I ask.

His response comes as a surprise: "Every Friday evening, my grandfather Amandus, a religious man and important role model for me, stopped by our house and took me with him to temple in Hamburg."

I suddenly understand that unlike many Jews who learned about their religion at home and can pass it on to the next generation through home-based rituals, my father's experience of Judaism is in synagogue (and in his bones). The only way he knows how to pass it on is to take his two sons to a Reform temple very different from the one of his childhood. All those years growing up, I *was* receiving a spiritual transmission, but Father didn't have the words to spell it out.

Reflection–Transformation

In Part One, I've shared stories about becoming a teacher using the framework of Thich Nhat Hanh's teachings on "transformation at the base," becoming aware of the seeds of our consciousness and choosing "what to do and what not to do," as Thầy often said. Influenced by this model of the world and the importance of watering wholesome seeds, I realized that my main goal as an educator was not just to teach mathematics or, later, to lead mindfulness retreats for educators, but to *facilitate change*—to help bring about a transformation of consciousness in myself and others.

Changes in consciousness are not brought about by arranging external causes and conditions. Transformation is affected by how we act amid change—which seeds we water. When I learned about the meaning my father placed on going to synagogue in Germany on Friday nights with his grandfather, it watered the latent seed of my own spirituality and helped me understand the deep connectedness I felt during Quaker meetings at Sidwell School.

Over time I learned that to facilitate transformation, we need to create settings that support self-confidence, and healthy, rewarding relationships. So I selected textbooks that students could easily learn from, and I organized small groups to create safe learning spaces. Later on I added time for reflection and contemplation.

This book is about the causes and the conditions in my life that have served in my transformation. Each experience, when I attend to it, supports understanding. My mindfulness practice informs my life, and my life informs my practice. The line between life events and formal practice dissolves as we water the seeds of becoming who we are.

Invitation

Sit in a comfortable position. Relax. Let your eyes close and breathe in and out slowly three times. Invite experiences of transformation into your awareness, notice what comes to mind, and reflect on how whatever it was has contributed to who you are today. When you feel ready, open your eyes.

PART TWO

SANGHA

If you are in a good community, one in which people are happy and living deeply each moment of their day, personal transformation will take place naturally, without effort. ... Two thousand five hundred years ago the Buddha Shakyamuni predicted that the next Buddha will be named Maitreya, the "Buddha of Love." I think the Buddha of Love may be born as a community and not as an individual. Communities of mindful living are crucial for our survival and the survival of our planet. A good Sangha can help us resist the speed, violence, and unwholesome ways of our time. ... We need the support of friends in the practice. You are my Sangha. Let us take good care of each other."

—Thich Nhat Hanh,
A Joyful Path: Community, Transformation, and Peace

Thầy's advice to participants in the June 1992 Plum Village retreat that the Sangha was the retreat's most important element came from fifty years of experience.[7] In Vietnam as in other Asian countries, the Sangha meant the monastic Sangha. When Thầy ordained as a novice, he joined a monastic family that traced its origins back to the Buddha. Thầy's written accounts of his early years reveal his connections with fellow monks and one nun, their friendship and their shared practice.

In 1964, as the American War wreaked destruction on the Vietnamese countryside, Thầy co-founded the School of Youth for Social Service (SYSS) in Saigon, training young people to help establish schools, provide medical care, and rebuild villages. The work was demanding and dangerous. Thầy saw the importance of the practice and community support offered by Sangha and began organizing weekly days of mindfulness for SYSS social workers and volunteers. Drawing on the leadership roles elders played in the monastic Sangha, Thầy ordained six members of the SYSS board into his new *Tiep Hien* order (Order of Interbeing) to serve as examples and teachers for the younger members. These new members vowed to practice fourteen precepts [Appendix 1]. When Thầy was unable to return to Vietnam in in the mid-1960s, he lost his homeland and a physical connection to his Sangha. In Paris, the small number of laypeople who supported his peace work became his Sangha.

The pace of life in the West, emphasis on success and attainment, sacrificing the present moment for the future, and the diminished role of the family heightened his awareness of the contribution Sangha and Buddhist teachings and practice could offer us. He began publishing his writings in English and teaching. From the beginning, Thầy encouraged his students to organize Sanghas to support their practice when they returned home from retreats. In fact, he told those who received the Five Precepts that their transmission would become null and void if they didn't recite them regularly with a Sangha. The Five Precepts, which later become known in Thich Nhat Hanh's tradition as the Five Mindfulness Trainings [Appendix 2], are ethical guidelines, first offered by the Buddha to his lay followers. They are completely compatible with other religions' tenets. When *The Mindfulness Bell*,[8] the international magazine for English-speaking students of Thich Nhat Hanh, began publication in 1990, each of its three yearly issues contained Sangha news and listings of Sanghas in North America and abroad,[9] helping some attenders of Thầy's retreats find Sanghas when they returned home. For the many who didn't have Sanghas back home, his retreats began to include sessions on Sangha building.

Lay Sanghas, like their monastic Sangha counterparts, are communities of like-minded individuals supporting each other to live more mindful and enlightened lives in order to relieve suffering and promote happiness for themselves and others. Most lay Sanghas in the Plum Village tradition practice sitting and walking meditation, read books or watch videos by Thầy and other Plum Village monastics, and practice Dharma sharing. Thầy often said that taking refuge in the Sangha is like a drop of water joining the ocean.

Plum Village offers the following guidelines for the profoundly connecting practice of Dharma sharing:[10] Sharing our experiences in a small group discussion is an opportunity to benefit from each other's insights and reflection. It is an opportunity to share our joys, difficulties, and questions about the practice of mindful living. By practicing deep listening while others are speaking, we help create a calm and receptive environment. By learning to speak out about our happiness and our challenges in the practice, we contribute to the communal insight and understanding of the Sangha.

We're encouraged to base our sharing on our own *experience* of the practice rather than abstract ideas or theoretical topics. Doing so, we discover the extent to which we share difficulties and aspirations. Sitting, listening, and sharing, we recognize the depth of our connections to one another. Whatever is shared during Dharma sharing is, of course, confidential.[11]

In the intimate setting of Dharma sharing, you may feel your full humanness as you are being listened to with 100 percent presence, and you have the opportunity to offer others the same.

Chapter 3

LIVING THE QUESTIONS

A tangerine has sections. If you can eat just one section, you can probably eat the entire tangerine. But if you can't eat a single section, you cannot eat the tangerine.

–Thich Nhat Hanh,
The Miracle of Mindfulness: A Manual on Meditation

The Eastern Stream

When I first looked at Pendle Hill's schedule of classes, Parker Palmer's spring-term course Monasticism in the Modern World didn't appeal to me. Now that I'm here, I understand that anything Parker teaches is gold. In his class, I'm absorbed by Thomas Merton's and Henri Nouwen's writings about their religious lives. Although I don't relate to their Christian roots, I see a connection between their aspirations and mine. Both men are creative, wide-ranging thinkers who are openly struggling to find their spiritual paths. "Monasticism in the Modern World" turns out to be my favorite course. Parker begins each class with a reading from Merton's *The Way of Chuang Tzu*. First we read the poem, then dwell on it in silence before writing in our journals. Finally, emerging out of the silence, we share. Chuang Tzu's messages of non-doing, non-thinking, and nowhere to go are balm for my active mind. They are disquieting as well. "The Woodcarver," Parker's favorite, continues to absorb me.

THE WOODCARVER

Khing, the master carver, made a bell stand
of precious wood. When it was finished,
all who saw it were astounded.
They said it must be
the work of spirits.
The Prince of Lu said to the master carver:
"What is your secret?"

Khing replied: "I am only a workman:
I have no secret. There is only this:
when I began to think about the work you commanded
I guarded my spirit, did not expend it
on trifles that were not to the point.
I fasted in order to set
my heart at rest.
After three days fasting,
I had forgotten gain and success.
After five days
I had forgotten praise or criticism.
After seven days
I had forgotten my body
with all its limbs.

"By this time all thought of your Highness
and of the court had faded away.
All that might distract me from the work
had vanished.

I was collected in the single thought
of the bell stand.

"Then I went to the forest
to see the trees in their own natural state.
When the right tree appeared before my eyes,
the bell stand also appeared in it, clearly, beyond doubt.
All I had to do was to put forth my hand
and begin.

"If I had not met this particular tree
there would have been
no bell stand at all.

"What happened?
My own collected thought
encountered the hidden potential in the wood;
from this live encounter came the work
which you ascribe to the spirits."[12]

This poem amplifies my experience of sitting in silence during Meeting for Worship and takes it out into the world. It leaves me wondering whether it is relevant to the life I'm living. I don't know it now, but this introduction to Eastern thought will eventually lead to a sea change in my life.

A New Interest

At a Pendle Hill community meeting, some retreatants request a day of silence. I participate, enjoying the space provided by refraining from talk. During the silent dinner, one of the organizers reads aloud a passage from Thầy's book *The Miracle of Mindfulness* about eating a tangerine with mindfulness.

EATING A TANGERINE

I remember a number of years ago, when Jim and I were first traveling together in the United States, we sat under a tree and shared a tangerine. He began to talk about what we would be doing in the future. Whenever we thought about a project that seemed attractive or inspiring, Jim became so immersed in it that he literally forgot about what he was doing in the present. He popped a section of tangerine in his mouth and, before he had begun chewing it, had another slice ready to pop into his mouth again. He was hardly aware he was eating a tangerine. All I had to say was, "You ought to eat the tangerine section you've already taken." Jim was startled into realizing what he was doing.

It was as if he hadn't been eating the tangerine at all. If he had been eating anything, he was "eating" his future plans.

A tangerine has sections. If you can eat just one section, you can probably eat the entire tangerine. But if you can't eat a single section, you cannot eat the tangerine. Jim understood. He slowly put his hand down and focused on the presence of the slice already in his mouth. He chewed it thoughtfully before reaching down and taking another section.

Later, when Jim went to prison for activities against the war [in Vietnam], I was worried whether he could endure the four walls of prison and sent him a very short letter: "Do you remember the tangerine we shared when we were together? Your being there is like the tangerine. Eat it and be one with it. Tomorrow it will be no more."[13]

Tending to the section of tangerine in my mouth, savoring it slowly and subtly, intrigues me. I learn that the reading comes from *The Miracle of Mindfulness* by Thich Nhat Hanh. I buy the book and take it home, where it remains unopened on my shelf.

Three years pass, and Elisabeth, sick in bed, asks me to read to her. I take that book from the shelf and begin to read. Immediately

I'm captivated by the first lesson on how to have unlimited time for oneself. I bring the book to school and begin reading it aloud for five minutes at the beginning of each math class. The students understand. When we complete it, they ask for more. I read *The Sun My Heart*, the sequel to *The Miracle of Mindfulness*. Reading these books, I feel they might as well be science fiction. They're about a life so radically different from the one I know. I don't know anyone who meditates, but Elisabeth, deeply involved in Quaker life, supports my interest.

Chris

Every spring our seniors undertake personal study projects during the three weeks prior to graduation. Afterward, they share their experiences with the faculty and younger students. For his senior project, Chris shares introductory teachings about meditation. He and a classmate had been studying Eastern religion and philosophy for six years, and the previous fall, he saw an announcement about newcomer evenings at the Zen Center of Washington, DC. "I decided to put my body where my mind was," he tells us. He continued to meditate there several evenings a week during the school year, then for his senior project, he helped at the Zen Center.

Chris describes his project with gusto, including a story about an intensive weekend retreat. Then he takes questions. One student observes, "It seems you're spending a lot of time sitting on a cushion now. Has your life changed in other ways?"

Chris pauses before answering, "Meditation has affected my life in many ways, most too subtle to even describe. What I can say is that I'm less angry."

Wow! His answer moves me, I'm deeply grateful. Thanking Chris afterward, I tell him the Zen Center isn't far from where I live, and I plan to visit it after returning from a summer on the West Coast.

Green Gulch

My first encounter with Zen comes sooner than I expected. In California with Elisabeth and our one-year-old daughter, Shoshanna, for the summer of 1988, I attend a Buddhist memorial service for a Quaker/Buddhist friend of Elisabeth's. Noting my interest in Buddhism and wanting to help me find my own spiritual path, Elisabeth, a California native, encourages me to ask about meditation groups. "This is California. You can find anything here," she tells me.

One of the mourners suggests Green Gulch Zen Center in Marin County. Several days later I board a bus for Green Gulch. The center is open to the public on Sunday mornings for meditation and instruction, a public lecture by one of the teachers, followed by a Q&A with the morning speaker, and a delicious vegetarian lunch. I'm also thinking about returning for several days. As soon as I attempt to sit *zazen* (formal seated meditation) on a meditation cushion for forty minutes with my spine erect, I'm taken with the physical discipline that's been missing from my life. I don't play sports or a musical instrument. I'm not sure why I would bother about a physical discipline, but just as I trust a leading in Meeting for Worship, I trust this impulse.

In his talk that morning, Zen priest Norman Fischer describes Zen as having three sequential components: the first is committing to zazen, whether it's one hour a week or several hours a day, and honor that commitment for weeks, months, or years. As a consequence of honoring that commitment, over time you begin to develop "one-pointed attention." Finally, after bringing this attention to your meditation over a period of years, you may discover answers to some of life's fundamental questions, for example, "Who am I?"

I wonder about my feelings of spiritual inspiration in Quaker worship at Sidwell Friends. I don't know how, or if, they fit into Norman's meditation practice. My sense is that they're different but related. Am I ready to commit?

After the talk, another member of the community makes an announcement: "Green Gulch is in the process of planning its next courses and invites visitors to identify Buddhist texts that are of particular interest." I wonder about this. Norman didn't include study as a component of Zen. At the informal discussion, I raise this question. Norman explains that at birth we receive a pair of metaphorical glasses with a prescription determined by our family, religion, culture, etc. Through these lenses we view our lives. As we study Buddhism, we discover that we are indeed wearing glasses. Study can help us remove the glasses and see life in a more authentic way, as it is. I'm reassured. My beginner's mind doesn't seem to put me at a disadvantage here. But will I find the transcendent dimension I'd discovered in Quaker worship? Is this path focused exclusively on moving toward some elusive Zen truth?

Return

A few weeks later, I return to Green Gulch for a three-day stay as a guest student. There I experience simple work, meditation, eating, and sleeping. I have an hour for study in the afternoons. The schedule with assigned chores and "single-selection" meals rules our lives. I'm focused on the moment, which is rare. The absence of outer freedom oddly promotes inner freedom. Although my usual regrets and anxieties are calmed, I still have to contend with self-judgment. *I'm doing a lousy job of hoeing. I'm not mindful when I wash the dishes. I don't sit still during zazen.* Sitting erect and motionless on a cushion from 5:30 a.m. until 6:10 a.m., continually counting my breath from one to ten and then backwards to one, I am trying.

Zazen requires a level of discipline far greater than any I've ever known. But whether I will ever develop deep insight or what they call one-pointed attention may be beside the point. I find the discipline of great value.

During one early morning period in the almost pitch-dark barn, as I sit on a cushion on a raised platform facing the wall, an itch wells up in my throat and grows in intensity. I know it will soon erupt in a coughing spell. In the deep silence I feel I can neither leave nor cough. During the ensuing struggle, I continue to breathe, doing my best to attend to each breath. Finally, my throat relaxes, without a cough! I feel totally at peace. This happens again the next day when my back seizes up, causing so much pain I think I'll fall over. After breathing and bearing it for a few minutes, that pain magically abates too. My sense of the connectedness of body, mind, and breath will never be the same.

The discipline of Japanese Soto Zen feels strangely familiar, as if it's the missing piece of my life, a welcome discovery! But how does this meditation fit in with my personal spiritual path? In this Soto Zen tradition, students are offered formal interviews, called *dokusan*, with a teacher. I ask to see Reb Anderson, the abbot of Green Gulch. After describing my experiences as a Jew and a Quaker, and my current encounter with Zen meditation, I say, "I don't know whether I'm Jewish, Quaker, or Buddhist."

"None of these," Reb replies. "The difference between being an attender and a member of a Quaker meeting is like the difference between living with someone and being married. You fall in love and live together. The relationship feeds both of you. Then one day you wake up and know you're not just in this for your own happiness and well-being. You're also in it for your lover's. Then you're ready to make a commitment. Spiritual paths are the same. You can be fed by one path or several. The time may come when you want to commit your life to one particular path."

"Thank you," I say. "That hasn't happened yet."

Thich Nhat Hanh

The experience at Green Gulch—discipline, living in the present moment, persevering through pain—convinces me to continue meditating when I return to Maryland. At the Zen Center of Washington, I don't feel a connection with the other meditators. I try sitting at home. My efforts are sporadic and unsatisfying. I stop trying and wonder if meditation is my path after all. Then, in the spring of 1989, Elisabeth shows me an announcement about Thich Nhat Hanh leading two five-day retreats on the East Coast in June, one at the Omega Institute in Rhinebeck, New York. Headmaster Earl Harrison generously gives me the week of commencement off.

With great anticipation, I drive up to New York.

Being with Thich Nhat Hanh in person, I find the buddha I didn't know I was looking for. As he gracefully walks, often holding hands with one or two children, I'm reminded of Jesus. The language of his Dharma talks is simple, the teachings spacious and profound. His

Thich Nhat Hanh
PHOTO BY SIMON CHAPUT

closing talk on interbeing and continuation describes the illusory nature of birth and death. Wow! This is all new. He tells us not to take notes, to just absorb the teachings as we might a gentle rain. If we take notes, we'll receive the teachings only in an intellectual way. He adds that just as with a massage you can receive the benefits of a Dharma talk even if you're asleep. Over the years since then, this has been my experience. Sometimes I fall asleep even when I'm not tired. The one sure-fire way I find to stay awake is to sit close to Thich Nhat Hanh where the energy field is intense.

Throughout this first retreat, whatever he says, I feel he's addressing me directly. Others tell me they have the same experience. We receive what is known as a transmission, his energy directly conveyed to us. It's clear! I'm ready to follow Thich Nhat Hanh's teachings, to embark on the path of mindfulness. At last I've found a path I can follow and truly commit to.

In a ceremony toward the end of the retreat, Thich Nhat Hanh transmits the Five Precepts, or basic rules of morality, and the Three Refuges. Often called the "Three Jewels," the Three Refuges are the Buddha, the Dharma, and the Sangha

To say "I take refuge in the Buddha," means that I strongly believe in my ability to transform my difficulties and be free from suffering so I can be a source of joy and peace for myself and others. To take refuge in the Buddha is to take refuge in the Buddha nature in myself, the innate potential for awakening. I take refuge in Buddha as a teacher of the way out of suffering, not as a god.

To say "I take refuge in the Dharma" means I practice mindfulness, which brings understanding and love. I believe in the method that Shakyamuni Buddha offered from his own experience to me so that I can realize the path that leads to freedom from suffering.

To say "I take refuge in the Sangha" means I believe in the collective wisdom of a group of friends who vow to practice as I do on our path of liberation. We need each other for support in this wonderful practice so our collective efforts will benefit ourselves and all beings.[14]

Although traditionally receiving the Three Refuges and the Five Precepts make one a "Buddhist," for Thầy that is not the case. He often emphasizes that practicing these tenets make one a better Christian, Muslim, or Jew. For me, the ceremony marks my personal commitment to Thich Nhat Hanh as my teacher and to his path.

Sangha

When Thầy transmits the Three Refuges, I vow to take refuge in the Buddha, the Dharma, and the Sangha. I have little idea what these vows look like or where they will lead me. Those of us who receive the Five Precepts agree to recite them every two weeks with a spiritual community, a Sangha. There is no Sangha in Thầy's tradition at home, but finding one turns out to be easy. On the final afternoon of the retreat, participants attend informal tea gatherings with others from their own region. Several of us from DC who have received the precepts want to start a Sangha. I offer to host the first gathering.

A couple of weeks later, six of us who attended the retreat at Omega or an earlier retreat Thich Nhat Hanh led in Virginia begin to practice together. Eventually we become known as the Washington Mindfulness Community (WMC). None of us has much previous experience with meditation, and our beginnings are somewhat shaky. The host for each session sets the schedule and chooses the reading. At one meeting, the host reads several of his poems that are offensive to others. Another evening, a different host accompanies our normally silent walking meditation with flute music. Some find it distracting. There are also special moments. One memorable evening at a member's high-rise apartment, we walk mindfully through the halls to the elevator and out onto the roof of the building. Outside, as we do walking meditation in the darkening evening, thunder and lightning from distant storms punctuate our breathing. I walk as if I'm in another world.

That fall, our group begins meeting at Chua Giac Hoang Temple, a Vietnamese Pure Land Buddhist temple in Northwest DC. We are invited to practice there by Venerable Thầy Giác Thanh, one of Thich Nhat Hanh's senior monks from Vietnam, who lives at the temple as a guest when he's away from Plum Village. Thầy Giác Thanh joins our practice and is a sweet addition to the group. During Dharma sharing, he frequently offers short, insightful talks, sometimes difficult to follow. His English isn't strong, but his presence is beautiful and nourishing.

Finally, after some tiffs about the format, we agree to follow a standard program based on Plum Village practice: silent sitting and walking meditation, recitation of the Five Precepts, listening to a portion of a recorded talk by Thich Nhat Hanh, and speaking from our personal experience, sharing our Dharma. We've learned from our retreat experience that sharing our personal Dharma includes sharing our suffering, our happiness, and our experience with the practice outside the meditation hall—challenges and successes. This level of vulnerability comes more easily to some than others. Over time the intimacy helps nourish the group energy and draw us together. I've entered a new spiritual stream, clear and sparkling, yet 2,600 years old.

Chapter 4

ALL IN THE FAMILY

If we do not know how to take care of ourselves and to love ourselves, we cannot take care of the people we love. Loving oneself is the foundation for loving another person.

–Thich Nhat Hanh,
Calming the Fearful Mind: A Zen Response to Terrorism

Meditating Alone at Home

My practice of mindfulness leads to new developments in our family. Encouraged by weekly meditations with the Sangha, I establish a daily sitting practice at home. I rise early, walk upstairs to the loft, and sit for half an hour. Instead of counting my breaths, I use the guided meditation Thich Nhat Hanh taught us at Omega:

Breathing in, I know I am breathing in.
Breathing out, I know I am breathing out.
Breathing in, my breath grows deep.
Breathing out, my breath grows slow.
Breathing in, I feel calm.
Breathing out, I feel ease in my body.
Breathing in, I smile.
Breathing out, I release.

Dwelling in the present moment,
I know it is a wonderful moment.[15]

It's a refreshing way to begin my day.

Shoshanna

After a few years, four-year-old Shoshanna climbs the stairs to the loft to find me sitting in silence. I greet her: "Please come and sit quietly on my lap for a few minutes while I finish meditating." Sometimes Shoshanna accepts. Other times she quietly returns downstairs and waits for me to finish. Soon an invitation is no longer needed.

When Shoshanna comes to me with a headache, I don't immediately try to "fix" it. I calmly invite her to breathe and be with her headache. Her headache begins to dissipate along with any anxiety. When we wash dishes together, she sees that I'm not in a hurry to finish. Thich Nhat Hanh teaches us to wash each dish as if it were the baby Buddha. Shoshanna sees that I give my full attention to washing.

Elisabeth

Bringing mindfulness practice to my relationship with Elisabeth is more challenging. Anger is my communication litmus test. My mother called my father's anger "unhelpful." In the early years of our marriage, I'm rarely in touch with emotions, especially anger. In due course, I begin to feel anger arise, but I don't want to poison our relationship, so I say nothing. My "good Buddhist" phase ends when I can no longer control my upset. I'm shocked when Elisabeth welcomes my angry words, asking only that I refrain from profanity. Unburdening myself of strong feelings provides relief in the moment but rarely helps resolve our issues. I begin waiting for my anger to subside before I speak. Some of the time this helps.

Thich Nhat Hanh asked that we not "rehearse" our anger, not even for five minutes. However, my attempts to reduce emotions to mere descriptions don't work for either of us. Eventually my anger and Elisabeth's anger become *just* anger, no longer threatening. I receive Elisabeth's anger calmly, with compassion, and I share my own awareness that it's an expression of pain that spans ancestral time.

When Elisabeth is upset, our encounters reflect this. At times she isn't conscious of being upset, or she may not be upset specifically with me. Still, her words and the tone of her voice when she corrects or instructs me trigger the tender child in me afraid of his father's ire. "I am not your father," Elisabeth says. However, at that moment, she *is* my father. As a child I shut down to my father's barbs, and I carry this habit into our marriage. Mindfulness practice helps. Eventually, I learn to stop, breathe, and then hold difficult childhood feelings in the larger container of mindfulness. Once I can feel compassion for my own suffering, I can ask Elisabeth what's troubling her and give her the attention she deserves.

Mom

When I learn that Thich Nhat Hanh will be giving a public lecture in Chicago during his 1991 North American tour, I encourage my mother to attend. My mom's mind—always curious and full of ideas—is anything but quiet. After she attends his teaching with a friend, I'm curious to hear her response.

"Did you like Thich Nhat Hanh?" I ask.

"Yes, he was very nice."

"Was there anything in particular about his talk you remember?"

"He gave us a meditation that included the words, 'Breathing in, I experience myself as still water; breathing out, I reflect things just as they are.' My eyes were closed, and suddenly I saw myself at midnight many years ago sitting silently with a fellow camper in a canoe in the middle of Blue Lake. The moon was reflecting on the calm water. It was so peaceful."

Mom's story moves me. Her memory is much like my own of the Camp Nebagamon bonfire. And now that she's met my teacher, she's entrusted her dream of peace to me.

Dad

That same year I reflect on my father's Alzheimer's. He's still living at home in Illinois, and I know his time for travel is limited. I call my mother and tell her I want to pick Dad up and fly with him to visit our California family. Since Mother is caring for my brain-damaged brother, Bob, as well, she knows she cannot make the trip.

At first Father is happy to travel. He and I fly to San Francisco, rent a car, and head for Aunt Ruth's. Then, without warning, he says he wants to go home.

"But we're going to Ruth's," I inform him. "We're in San Francisco."

"I don't want to go there. I want to go home," he replies. There's no arguing. He is clear. I realize I must agree.

"We can go home, but there are no more flights to Chicago this evening," I tell him. "Tomorrow morning I'll call the airline, change our tickets, and we'll fly home."

This satisfies him. When he wakes up the next morning, there's no talk of going home.

The highlight of our trip is dinner at a German restaurant with Ruth and my father's cousins. The relatives are happy to see my much-loved father. In fine fettle, Dad relates childhood stories, some several times. The evening is boisterous and gay. Afterward, back at Ruth's house, Father says, "I don't know who those people were, but they knew all the old stories." I smile a happy-sad smile.

Realizing that travels with my father might be taxing, Elisabeth encourages me to think about how to take care of myself. At her suggestion I call her friend Cara, who lives in San Francisco, and we set a date for a walk. Cara has been practicing Tibetan Buddhism for some time and confirms a new inner knowing she sees in me now that I've found a teacher who touches my deepest self. Cara tells me my life will never be the same. "You'll receive all future teachings in the context of his guidance. He is a heart teacher: When you meet him, you can only ask, 'What have I done in my life to deserve such trainings?'" I don't see this yet. Cara's wisdom seeds will take time to bear fruit. How refreshing, though, to hear what she has to say.

Past Life

It's the next summer. Mom has moved Dad from our family home in Glencoe, Illinois, to a nursing home not far from where my family lives in Maryland. One morning I ride my bike across Rock Creek Park to Elise's house for a massage. Lying face down on her table, I hear low Gregorian chants in the background. Tired and grateful, I feel her soothing hands on my back. As my consciousness drops down, the time and place suddenly change; the hands I feel are not Elise's but my father's. It's the time of the Inquisition. I've been flogged to death and have risen to heaven where my father greets me. He gently massages my lacerated skin, helping me shed it. My vision is clear; this is not a dream. It continues for some time. Eventually my consciousness returns to Elise's room and to her hands. That afternoon I visit Dad. Although we speak little, I sense a connection stronger than I've ever felt before. Is it related to the morning vision? I have no idea. Past-life experiences are not my usual reality. I tell Elisabeth about my vision, then file it away.

All the while I attend weekly meditations and other gatherings of the Washington Mindfulness Community. A few new people join, and some of the original members depart. Our Sunday evening meditation draws anywhere from three to fifteen people. Thanks in part to Thich Nhat Hanh's nearby lectures and retreats, which WMC helps plan and support every other year, our local Sangha grows. By the time Thầy Giác Thanh leaves in 1993, to reside year-round at Plum Village, there's a core group of ten members for Sunday evening practice. We're all Westerners, with no previous experience of Buddhism. Many of us long to deepen our practice. One of our early members, Mitchell Ratner, travels to France to attend the 1991–92 Winter Retreat in Plum Village. Hearing Mitchell's account of Plum Village upon his return, I want to go there, too.[16] I depart as soon as school ends in June 1992 to attend the biennial three-week retreat which attracts senior practitioners from around the world.

Reflection—Sangha

Sangha, according to Thich Nhat Hanh, is a critical element of the path of transformation. Sharing mindfulness practices and the energies of volition and commitment with others provides optimal conditions for growth, more effective than solo practice and study. Presence and connection among Sangha members, nurtured by deep listening and loving speech, lead to understanding and friendship. Held by the container of silence, our suffering and happiness become our Sangha's suffering and happiness.

Thầy described Sangha as "an organism," always moving, changing, and growing to meet new circumstances. In a loving Sangha, it is easy to transform the feeling of separation into connection. To help newcomers feel at home, the Washington Mindfulness Community adopted second-body practice, a kind of buddy system borrowed from the Plum Village monastics. Every three months interested WMC members were given second bodies with whom they could meet weekly to share their experience with practice. These opportunities, in concert with Dharma discussion, profoundly changed the depth of practice for many members who joined the WMC after practicing at home alone.

As your practice matures, not only the mindfulness community but family, colleagues, and friends can become your Sangha.

Although they may not be practitioners, they suffer and aspire to well-being and happiness too. Over time compassionate listening, loving speech, and the willingness to be vulnerable water these same seeds in them.

Invitation

Sit in a comfortable position. Relax. Let your eyes close and breathe in and out slowly three times. Invite your experience of community into your awareness. Simply notice whatever experiences, feelings, or thoughts related to *Sangha* come to mind. Reflect on the impact they have had on your sense of safety and well-being in the world. When you feel ready, open your eyes.

PART THREE

IMPERMANENCE

Thanks to impermanence, everything is possible.

–Thich Nhat Hanh,
*Awakening of the Heart: Essential Buddhist
Sutras and Commentaries*

Thầy frequently illustrated impermanence with the image of a wave. A wave *appears* to begin somewhere on the ocean, travel for a while, sometimes a long while, and eventually comes to an end. What we are actually seeing are progressive droplets of water moving in cyclic patterns. The water in a wave at any moment is different from that of the previous moment. Thầy said that the word "wave" is just a term to describe this action of water, usually caused by wind. Likewise, "Richard Brady" is a conventional designation for a particular collection of cells existing at this moment and changing in the next, as millions of cells are born while others die. When a wave "dies," the water remains. As for my death, my "water" is the subject of the fifth of the Buddha's Five Remembrances:

THE FIVE REMEMBRANCES

1) I am of the nature to grow old. There is no way to escape growing old.

2) I am of the nature to have ill health. There is no way to escape ill health.

3) I am of the nature to die. There is no way to escape death.

4) All that is dear to me and everyone I love are of the nature to change. There is no way to escape being separated from them.

5) I inherit the results of my actions of body, speech, and mind. My actions are my continuation.

Our thinking, speaking, and bodily actions—our karma—produce our continuation in "all forms of life." Monastics recite the Five Remembrances as part of their daily practice.[17] While the first four are historical-dimension truths, the fifth is an ultimate-dimension truth that can assuage our primal fear of the first four.

Thầy often said that without impermanence, we could never grow up and become our present selves. Many of us come to mindfulness practice seeking change. Increased awareness of the seeds we carry in our store consciousness may not produce the change we seek. But over time, practice leads to more equanimity, creating a field in which the transformation of unwholesome seeds is increasingly likely.

Plum Village and other practice centers provide an environment that supports being mindful twenty-four seven. Everything becomes a meditation. Further, the presence of experienced practitioners is a constant encouragement and reminder. We already know how to practice mindfulness; we just need encouragement and reminders to stay with ourselves and what is happening around us. For example, when we're listening to music, being with the natural world, or focusing on the ripe pear we're eating, we feel at peace. But these moments arise intermittently. On retreat, we aspire to bring mindfulness to whatever we're engaged in and to return to it when distractions arise. With the support of the community, there is less competition from seeds like judgment, anxiety, anger, and regret, and our seed of mindfulness grows.

When we return home, old seeds continue to sprout in mind-consciousness, but the lessons we practiced at the retreat center are also in our store consciousness and grow as we remember and practice with them. Sometimes we are the last to notice that we're changing, but over time we begin to see our mindful thoughts, words, and actions ripple out into the universe. And we then can see that the ocean that we are—our relationships with family, friends, colleagues, and our spiritual community—continuing us now and doing so into the future.

Chapter 5

HOMECOMING

"I have arrived, I am home." My home is right here
in the present moment.

—Thich Nhat Hanh and Katherine Weare,
Happy Teachers Change the World

Retreat

Plum Village is a watershed for me. Few monastics are present, but many senior lay practitioners from Europe, the US, and Asia attend this 1992 twenty-one-day retreat. Thầy tells us that the presence of the Sangha is "the main thing," not his teachings or the practice. Nonetheless, I find his teachings are markedly deeper and more intimate at this retreat than the ones he offered at Omega. He begins his first Dharma talk with a story of falling in love with a nun when he was a young monk in Vietnam. As he gradually unfolds his own love story over the three-week retreat, he intersperses it with teaching from the Diamond Sutra,[18] Lotus Sutra,[19] and Avatamsaka Sutra.[20] Many parts of these teachings mystify me, particularly the descriptions of the *avatamsaka* realm of lion seats, multicolored clouds, and lotus flowers in each of whose petals a thousand lotuses bloom.

I relax and let what Thầy calls the "Dharma rain" of the teachings soak in. I don't feel the need to take notes. Thầy's nonverbal teaching is particularly moving. Before Dharma talks, he pours himself a cup of tea and drinks it with total attention, then turns his gaze to us— very much like the story of the Buddha silently holding a flower before his monastics assembled at Vulture Peak to hear him speak until one of his disciples, Mahakasyapa, smiles, understanding that appreciating the flower *is* the lesson.

We have periods of sitting meditation in the mornings and in the evenings when there are no programs. We have a long outdoor walking meditation after Dharma talks, mindful eating in silence during all meals, working meditation doing jobs we volunteer for, and Dharma discussion in home groups several times each week. At other times, we're free to converse, meditate on our own, journal, or do whatever we choose.

One day each week is a "Lazy Day," an unscheduled day where meals are served, but practice is in our hands. Without the support of a schedule and the Sangha, these days present the greatest challenge to my practice. After a Lazy Day of doing little more than laundry, I begin to schedule half-day walks with people I've met and want to get to know better. This is how I make my first friend there, David Levy, a Xerox researcher from Palo Alto, California. I'm grateful to find a fellow practitioner with an interest in technology and its impact on society. Bright, caring, and thoughtful, David is a wonderful comrade for a long Lazy Day walk.

The retreat's program fits me to a T, but this isn't the case for everyone. During my group's first Dharma discussion, sharing experiences of the teachings "from the heart," a woman who is used to the narrower focus on silent formal practice in other Buddhist traditions says that this is her first involvement with Thich Nhat Hanh's tradition, and "If I had wanted to go on a vacation, I'd have gone to the beach."[21] Sadly, by the retreat's end she feels the same way. I witness that everyone's heart's desire is not always the same, that we have different needs at different times, and need different "medicine" for the ways we're hurting.

Past Life Redux

Sister Jina had come to Plum Village two years earlier after ordaining as a novice in Japan. This Plum Village nun of Dutch and Irish descent with a twinkle in her eye announces that monastic and experienced lay practitioners are available for one-on-one consultations. If we tell her the nature of our concern, she offers to connect us with an appropriate match. I wonder if I'm in the right place to find help understanding last year's past-life vision. Past lives are part of Buddhism, and there are many stories of the Buddha's former lives. Sr. Jina suggests I talk to Christopher Reed, a tall British Dharma teacher who directs the Ordinary Dharma Center in Venice, California. Christopher listens to my story then replies:

"Richard, your vision was what we call a mental formation, something that occurred in your mind. All formations, both mental and physical, manifest when causes and conditions are sufficient for them to do so. Innumerable causes and conditions went into the event you just described. You were tired; your friend was massaging your back. Your father, much on your mind, was a Jewish refugee from the Holocaust. You were hearing a Gregorian chant. These and countless other invisible reasons caused your vision and led to your perception of it as a past-life regression. Someone else living through such an experience might understand it differently. That you received the vision is a significant reflection of where you are on your path. The content is less important. You needn't dwell on it."

I understand Christopher and thank him for sharing his wisdom. I feel relieved and can let the idea of past lives go. However, that night I realize Christopher said nothing about the reality of reincarnation. Did the Buddha live countless lives or didn't he? Has anyone lived more than once? I need another consultation. The following day Christopher responds to these new questions.

"All we know about the Buddha's past lives comes from his teachings. No one else can know what the Buddha actually lived.

No one else can know what happened to you. They can only hear your words and see your actions. We do know that the Buddha was one of the world's great teachers. We also know that he gave his teachings to Hindu people, in the context of Hindu society, people for whom past lives were quite real. Whatever the Buddha's experience, it is not surprising that he employed teachings that would speak to his students."

Coming from so many years of my own experience as a high school math teacher, I appreciate the skill of bearing in mind the nature of one's students.

Order of Interbeing

During the same retreat, I'm fortunate to get a consultation with Joan Halifax, a respected Dharma teacher and anthropologist who works with the terminally ill. Elisabeth and I have discussed cremation, and I want to know the Buddhist view. Joan tells me it is frequently part of Buddhist funerals. As our conversation ends, Joan looks at her watch and says it's time for us to go to the meeting.

"What meeting?" I ask.

"The OI meeting," she replies.

I know that "OI" refers to the Order of Interbeing, a monastic and lay order created in Vietnam in 1966 by Thich Nhat Hanh.

"Aren't you an OI member?" Joan asks.

I am not. It dawns on me then that the brown jackets Joan, Christopher, and other senior practitioners wear are not just Plum Village fashion but indicative of their membership in the OI. When I attended my first retreat with Thầy three years earlier, I had purchased his book *Interbeing: Fourteen Guidelines for Engaged Buddhism*. It explains the fourteen precepts received by OI members and describes the role and expectations of the order. At that time, I couldn't conceive of myself joining the OI or any "order." Three years later, back in my Plum Village dorm room, I find a copy of *Interbeing* left on the floor by my bed. Picking it up, I reread it with new eyes. The Order is a family of elder sisters and brothers, the kind of family that I, the elder brother of my birth family and now, once again, an elder brother in WMC Sangha, yearn for. Might I join?

Sister Chan Khong has been at Thich Nhat Hanh's side since 1964 when she returned from her studies in Paris to assist him in founding and administering the School of Youth for Social Service. She is the person who receives requests on Thầy's behalf. When I query her about becoming an OI member, she asks, "Have you been practicing with this intention with your Sangha for a year?"

"No," I reply. "I formed my intention yesterday."

"Then go home and begin to practice with this intention," she tells me.

This is not the instant *yes* I had hoped for. Undaunted by Sr. Chan Khong's authority, I decide to get a second opinion and seek out my friend Therese Fitzgerald. Therese and her husband Arnie Kotler coordinate all of Thầy's retreats, days of mindfulness, and public lectures in the US. I and other members of the Washington Mindfulness Community worked with them on Thầy's previous retreat in Virginia. "This is Plum Village. Anything can happen here," Therese says, smiling. "Go ahead and write Thầy a letter telling him your aspiration and asking to join the Order. The worst that can happen is that your request will be turned down." I write a letter and drop it in the large bell in the meditation hall, Thầy's "mailbox."

Yes

A couple of days later, Thầy Giác Thanh, the monk I know from Washington, finds me after breakfast and invites me to take a walk. Ambling together through a grassy field, we are at peace. Quietly, he says, "Thầy does not feel you are ready to join the Order."

Of course not, I think. I need to go home, as Sr. Chan Khong advised, and practice with my intention.

Thầy Giác Thanh continues, "He feels you do not have enough joy in your life or support from your family."

It is true that the past year has been difficult, but how does Thầy know that? Then I recall having tea with Thầy in a small group before a Dharma talk. He asks each of us to tell him something about our practice. Jeanne, who sits to my left, tells of trying to kill herself seventeen times. On this retreat she has found the first peace she has ever experienced. Later another woman shares that she doesn't have anything special to say and suggests we each turn to the person next to us and smile. All I can see on Jeanne's face is her suffering. Neither of us smiles. Thầy sees this. As for family support, I came to Plum Village with Elisabeth's blessing, but she has never attended our Sangha. Does Thầy know this?

"I understand," I tell Thầy Giác Thanh. "I will work on these things."

"You might be ready to join the Order when Thầy visits the US next year," he suggests.

How much easier it would be to practice as a member of the OI family, I think.

I write Thầy a letter thanking him for considering my request. In it I include two *gathas* (mindfulness verses) I've written. The first is inspired by Sr. Jina:

Your smile is like a bell of mindfulness.
When I see it, I touch my own inner joy.

In Plum Village bells of all sorts, from the resounding sound of the large temple bell to the chimes every fifteen minutes of the clock in the dining area, are invitations to stop whatever we're doing, come back to ourselves, and listen deeply. All are referred to as "bells of mindfulness." Thầy has given us a gatha to recite silently to support this practice:

Listen, listen:
this wonderful sound

brings me back
to my true home.[22]

Here, "true home" refers to the here and now.

The second of my gathas was prompted by long waits in meal lines at the retreat:

Standing in this line,
I know my nonself is being served.

In Buddhism, *nonself* refers to nonduality—absence of the separate existence of all entities, which are entirely composed of ever-changing nonself elements, e.g., a flower is composed of the sun, the rain, the soil, its parent flower, etc. Likewise, those being served are part of me, and I am part of them. And the food will soon be a part of me, too.

I also include a poem I wrote on retreat as the first days of rain gave way to sunny skies.

The sun dries my muddy understanding.
Cracks develop in the firm earth.

Later in the retreat, to my surprise, Thầy relates a passage from the Lotus Sutra: In response to the Buddha, the ground of Gridhrakuta Mountain, Vulture Peak, cracks, and myriads of bodhisattvas (awakened beings) emerge. Have I somehow intuited this teaching?

I conclude my letter to Thầy with a joke that fellow retreatant John Bloss, a British peace worker in Sarajevo, and I had made up a few days earlier, playing off Thầy's teaching from the Diamond Sutra about transcending pairs of opposites such as birth and death and being and nonbeing:

An ancient scroll written in Pali was discovered in a cave in Sri Lanka. It was determined to be a heretofore unknown Sutra of the Buddha's and was given to Thầy to translate. Thầy translated it as the "Bagel Sutra." In it, the Buddha taught that the bagel has no beginning, no end, and no middle.

Several evenings later, Therese taps me on the shoulder and tells me she has good news: In the following morning's ceremony, I am to be ordained into the Order of Interbeing. My heart beats hard. No one back home knows. I try unsuccessfully to call Elisabeth and then Mitchell, my Dharma brother in DC. The next day, I carry Elisabeth and Shoshanna in my heart to the ceremony and silently repeat "Elisabeth" and "Shoshanna" with each in-breath and out-breath. Thầy gives me the Dharma name "True Dharma Bridge," which perfectly captures my wish to share his teachings. My decision to ordain seems sudden, but, I've been preparing to take this step ever since meeting Thầy three years ago. Now my heart feels ready.

Other Gifts

During our daily outdoor walking meditation, we usually stop for short periods of sitting or mindful movements. One day our leader asks each of us to silently find a partner. As we stand with our partner, the leader asks us to look at our hands.

"These hands have been with you since before your birth. They've served you your entire life. The story of your days and years, your joys, your sorrows—all of these are present in your hands."

Following the next direction, my partner offers me one of her hands. I gently hold it in mine. For three long minutes, I slowly sense what this hand has to tell me about her life. Then we switch and she reads the story of my life in my hand. We came together as strangers. Suddenly we know each other in a way no other living being does.

Another gift is my discovery of a special friend. At first I'm simply aware of her—quiet and often alone. I have no idea who she is, but I come to feel that we're meant to meet. For that to happen, I must take the initiative. One evening I approach her, introduce myself, and tell her I've had a sense we should meet. When she asks me what I think that's about, I have to admit I have no idea. Nel is a Dutch body therapist who lives in a mountain cottage above Zurich. On the surface we seem to have little in common. We have several deep conversations and later begin to correspond. Not having grown up with a sister, it takes me a while to recognize Nel as my spiritual sister. After meeting her in Plum Village the following year, Elisabeth tells me sagely, "Richard, if you'd been born a woman, that's who you'd be."

Dying

My time in Plum Village has been so rich that I feel ready to return home a few days ahead of schedule. What more can happen? The morning after a full moon ceremony which continued late into the night, I realize that if I don't take a nap after breakfast, I will likely sleep through Thầy's Dharma talk. My dorm room is empty. I feel a gentle breeze and hear the songs of birds as I prepare to lie down. I sink into my pillow with a peace so deep that I feel as though I'm dying. Images from the past parade through my consciousness. How can this be? I'm young and in good health, yet I know I'm about to die. *What a perfect place to die*, I think. Continuing to sink into my bed with death coming ever closer, I realize that Shoshanna and Elisabeth are not by my side. Without them I'm not ready to die.

I stop my descent with my elbows and raise my body out of the bed as two roommates enter. Shaking and shaken, I rise and walk out into the sunshine. Fortunately, Thầy Giác Thanh is standing outside my door. He scoops me into a big hug. He can feel my fear. "You've been given a chance to taste what it's like to let go," he tells me.

What's happening? My family isn't here, yet I'm surrounded by a group of new brothers and sisters. With my history, opening for support involves a big risk. When did I even see Dad or Mom ask the other for help? Little by little, I'm letting go of the intergenerational pattern of self-sufficiency.

Chapter 6

LIFE LESSONS

Don't go home as a Buddhist. Go home as a Buddha.[23]

—Thich Nhat Hanh

Lessons from Dad

Father's progressive Alzheimer's absorbs my attention. Mom has moved him to a nursing home near us in Maryland, and she moves to a nearby apartment. Dad is no longer predictable. Mom hears from his nursing home that he's begun wandering into a neighbor's room and lying down in her bed. Is this okay with Mom? "Yes, if it's okay with the woman." My relationship with my father changes. Now he only vaguely recognizes me. No longer conscious of his fatherly role, he's softer in my presence. I stand behind him, massage his shoulders, hold his hand, tell him I love him. My mother, always the caregiver, spends much of her time visiting him at his nursing home, making herself useful: the usual—Mom giving, not receiving. She seems unable to enjoy the gifts my father offers us, his lessons about life. I'd like to express this to her but don't know how. When I return from Plum Village, the words show up in the form of a story which appears in the nursing home's newsletter and later in the *Mindfulness Bell*. Mother tells me she appreciates it, but that is the end of our conversation. We never discuss it again.

Present Moment, Wonderful Moment

When I was growing up, my father taught me honesty, loyalty, generosity, and attention to detail, to name just a few life lessons he offered, mostly implicitly. Now, at age seventy-nine, he lives in a nearby nursing home and has Alzheimer's disease.

Dad recognizes almost nothing of the past. He can hardly access his long-term memory, cannot retain the recent past, and makes no plans for the future. Spending time with him forces me to dwell in the deep presence of each moment. That's all there is, and it's often a waterslide. Relieved of the possibility of cogent conversation, I hold his hand, massage his neck, walk with him, and play with my daughter, Shoshanna, now nearly four. My father seems content to watch with no need to join in our play.

To him I'm no longer anyone special. "Who is Richard Brady?" he asks. Sometimes I'm his son, but often I'm just another visitor. Without expectations, I'm allowed to be whichever Richard Brady arises in that moment. It seems to work *for him*, but I'm having a much harder time accepting this new reality. When he smiles and responds to me, I feel at ease. But when he stares into space or naps through our visits or fumes out of all proportion when accidentally bumped, old buttons are pushed, and I wrestle with my anger and the need for him to be other than he is.

He constantly shows me my dependence on the past—my notion of home, for example. During his recent visit to my house, the two of us took a walk. When we got back, I said, "Let's go in."

"No!" he replied adamantly, "I don't know the people who live here."

Luckily Shoshanna spotted us through the window, opened the door, and invited us in. Always a new person to my father, she is "wonderful," a child whose invitation he would never refuse. When we returned to the nursing home, I simply suggested, "Let's stop here. This looks like a nice place."

"Yes," he said. "Let's stop here."

He lets go of feelings as easily as he lets go of knowing. One minute he's enjoying a visit with us, and the next he's uncomfortable and ready to go. It's hard for me to flow with his inconsistencies, but as I learn to be with him, however he is, I discover that whether trying or pleasing, any feeling is impermanent, subject to change. No matter how slowly I drive, he wants me to go more slowly. When I do, he relaxes.

A few days after a recent visit to his nursing home, Elisabeth tells me she wishes I would sit and beam at her as I do at my father. Thanks to Dad, I'm learning to be completely present with another person, without language, past, or future.

Depression

Life lessons continue the following year, 1993, in a year-long meditation/therapy group. The year begins and ends with weekend retreats. In between, we meet monthly for an entire day. When I sign up, I have no idea that the therapy component will be psychodrama. Once during the year, I am the focus person, the protagonist, which means the group enacts an incident from my life. One person plays me.

The theme of my psychodrama is my childhood sense of invisibility and isolation. As I watch the players, I'm overwhelmed, even after the drama ends. Joy disappears, and my life becomes two-dimensional. On the edge of depression, I know I need the help of a therapist. I ask friends to recommend someone who draws on Eastern wisdom. Two of them recommend Rudy Bauer, a therapist and yoga practitioner.

After hearing about my suffering at our first session, Rudy asks me to identify someone I love unconditionally. "My daughter, Shoshanna," I readily reply. Rudy asks me to bring Shoshanna into my heart and feel the support of her presence. We focus awareness on energy in my body. He guides me here, then there, asking for feedback. He says, "Tolerate this, tolerate that, just tolerate it, don't think, don't judge," and several times, "It's no big deal." I begin to get back in touch with my loving self. Rudy explains afterward that working with old wounds may be the right thing to do in the future. But, he adds, my center is currently so weak I could easily become overwhelmed by emotion. As Rudy sees it, his job is to help me become emotionally grounded.

I visit Rudy weekly for five months. Our work is frequently meditative in nature, Rudy always maintaining energetic contact. Though my eyes are closed, I can feel his presence. Once he climbs up behind me on the sofa, presses his knees into my back, and pulls my shoulders backward. For ten minutes he holds me in this position to help me tune into my strength. Another time he connects me with my passion by asking me to close my eyes and listen to Indian devotional chants. "As you listen," Rudy instructs, "don't visualize anyone outside yourself as the source of your passion. Your passion is in you. It's not dependent on anyone else." Another meditation puts me in touch with my inner spaciousness.

My depression slowly lifts, and Rudy invites me to attend one of his groups. When I arrive at a session feeling joyless, Rudy asks three group members to grab my arms and waist and pull in different directions. Trying to resist, I erupt in screams that turn into belly laughter. Here is my body's hidden joy! None of the work with Rudy ever touches on the "historical material" that led me to see him in the first place. Later I'll be ready to encounter the past on my own.

Mom Redux

By 1993 it's been ten years since my last sabbatical, and I feel ready for another extended leave from Sidwell. Granted a leave of absence from teaching, I plan to go to Plum Village after Christmas to participate in six weeks of the three-month winter retreat. It will be a long time away from Shoshanna and Elisabeth. We decide the separation might be easier if we can all stay at Plum Village beforehand. We'll attend the annual summer opening, which draws many families. Shoshanna will be six years old.

I prepare by attending a spring retreat on transformation at the Kripalu Center for Yoga and Health in Lenox, Massachusetts. At the retreat, I attend *satsang* with Gurudev, Kripalu's spiritual leader. Devotees dressed in white sit in the front close to their teacher. I settle in just behind them. Gurudev begins to play plaintive, hypnotic music on the harmonium, creating a sort of trance state among us. Then he asks for questions. I have one, as do a number of devotees in front of me. I raise my hand and look Gurudev in the eye after he answers each query. Finally, he nods to me. Thinking about my inability to communicate my insights to my mom, I say, "I've received great benefit from my spiritual practice. How can I share it with my mother?"

"You know the answer," Gurudev replies. I sit in silence, confused and upset. Does Gurudev know about my mother's experience with Thich Nhat Hanh? Has he nothing more to say to me? Finally, he speaks again. "Go and wash her car."

I'm taken aback. The thought that I might have nothing of my precious spiritual path to offer her saddens me. I hope my upcoming visit to Plum Village will yield a more felicitous answer.

Brothers

I first hear of Plum Village during my 1989 retreat with Thầy at Omega Institute. A woman in our Dharma discussion group tells us that this is her first experience with meditation. Even though her life is happy and she has no history of trauma, she finds herself crying every time she meditates. If this is what meditation is like, she's not sure she wants to continue. People share with her that crying is not unusual. One says, with a bit of humor, that in Plum Village there's a rule against crying for more than five minutes. It's not uncommon, he adds, to find Westerners sobbing in the bushes.

That summer of 1993, when our family visits Plum Village for two weeks, I, too, find myself in tears. The setting is Dharma discussion. During a previous sharing, a retreatant named James says that ever since his arrival in Plum Village he's been carrying the weight of the world on his shoulders. He cannot account for it. During a question-and-answer session with Thầy the following day, James reveals that his brother committed suicide. He asks Thầy for advice. Thầy tells him that in each of us is the seed of suicide and the seed of joy. Which seed sprouts depends on which one we water. He adds that from what James has shared, it's clear that his seed of suicide has been thoroughly watered. James is at risk. He needs to carefully examine his home, his job, his friends, his life choices, and change any elements that are not watering his seed of joy.

That evening our Dharma discussion group meets again. This time there are just three of us—James, William, and me. Our discussion soon turns to James's sharing with Thầy the previous day. He tells us that earlier in his life he had a problem with alcohol. His sister-in-law was the only person who supported him. It was this sister-in-law who took her own life during a period of depression following her husband's suicide, leaving two small children behind. We listen deeply with compassion.

Next William tells us the story of his brother, a doctor. Two years earlier, his brother developed an aggressive brain tumor, and William booked a flight to visit him. The tumor had darkened his brother's mood considerably, and his brother told him not to come. With ticket in hand, William decided to ignore his brother's wishes. At the end of the long flight, a grief-stricken nephew met William. William's brother, pessimistic about the future of the world, had just killed his wife and himself.

We share a profound, extended silence. Tears fall. This suffering is more than personal, more than the suffering of a generation. It rises up in the blood from our ancestors, suffering that has been denied, hidden behind stern and proper behaviors, held at bay by living lives cut off from feeling. Here, now, this suffering has poured into the open. As night deepens around us, the anguish is inescapable.

Next I share the story of my brother Bob, my only sibling. As a teenager, he had a series of physical and psychological problems. Eventually Bob's condition led him to drop out of school, leave our home in Illinois, and move to California where he hoped to regain his health. He ate fresh fruit and vegetables, took supplements, and exercised but was unsuccessful. After returning home, Bob became attracted to fasting as a way to cleanse his body of toxins. He traveled to a health center in Texas to begin a supervised water fast. After forty-five days the medical staff advised Bob to stop. Unwilling to follow their advice, he continued for fifteen more days. Two days after completing his fast, Bob went into a coma. He came out of the coma with a stiff hip and brain damage that severely impaired his short-term memory and left him subject to seizures. Since then, Bob has lived with our parents or in one of several communities for people with mental disabilities. He refers to this experience as his first life, his death, and his second life. My sharing with James and William is the first time I've told my brother's story and been able to feel my grief deeply.

The three of us sit, holding our shared suffering. Through our tears, we contact a truth beyond suffering. From Thầy's teachings, we know how to embrace and cradle our pain as we would a crying baby. Whatever liberation we may find through our practice, we will share with the next generation: James with his young niece and nephew as well as his own son; William with his son and his grown nephews; I with my daughter. We are in Plum Village, home to scores of joyful monks and nuns, many of them Vietnamese refugees who have experienced the torment of war and emigration in their young lives. Thầy has taught them how to water the seeds of joy and how to embrace their distress. In the depth of our connection with the monastics and with each other, in the throes of anguish, we too find joy.

Father Transitions

I return home from Plum Village to discover that my father's condition has worsened. He's now bedridden most of the time, and he's stopped speaking. Because I'm on sabbatical, I'm able to visit him often. By mid-November, he is comatose. One evening I receive a call from his nursing home suggesting I come, that Father might not live through the night. I take a copy of Thầy's book, *Touching Peace*, which includes the Buddha's teachings on the historical and ultimate dimensions. In the historical dimension, we are separate beings who are born, grow older, and die. But in the ultimate dimension, we're ever-changing formations in a single interconnected reality, we *inter-are*. Thầy uses the analogy of waves that manifest when causes and conditions are sufficient and break when they cease to be so. In the historical dimension, individual waves are born and die. In the ultimate they are always water.

Reading the Chapter "Realizing Ultimate Reality" will be a comfort to me. In my father's room I find Mother and the wonderful night nurse, Daw Than Mya, whom Mom has told me about. Her freshness is a sweet surprise. I know she's been working with dementia patients for years. She asks about my book, then tells me she grew up in Thailand where she lived for a year as a renunciant. Now she and her husband make regular visits to the Bhavana Retreat Center in West Virginia, where her husband built a small meditation hut. Perhaps I've stayed in your hut, I tell her, enjoying the presence and warmth she brings to the room.

As my father's breathing becomes more labored, my mother and I sit on either side of him, holding his hands in ours. Slowly his breath stops. He has moved on, but I continue to feel his presence. He is still in me as he has always been. But the father I have carried inside me is no longer overshadowed by my flesh-and-blood father. A few days later we accompany his body to San Francisco to be buried near his brother, parents, and uncles. At my invitation, David Levy, my friend from Plum Village, attends the burial and gives me spiritual support.

This contemplation on the ultimate dimension of reality, chanted at cremations and burials in the Plum Village tradition, provides me a measure of comfort. We never die, it just appears so:

CONTEMPLATION ON NO-COMING, NO-GOING

This body is not me.
I am not limited by this body.
I am life without boundaries.
I have never been born,
and I have never died.
Look at the ocean and the sky filled with stars,
manifestations from my wondrous True Mind.
Since before time, I have been free.
Birth and death are only doors through which we pass,
sacred thresholds on our journey.
Birth and death are a game of hide and seek.
So laugh with me,
hold my hand, let us say goodbye,
say goodbye, to meet again soon.
We meet today.
We will meet again tomorrow.
We will meet at the source at every moment.
We meet each other in all forms of life.[24]

A month later, just after Christmas, I leave for Plum Village. There I am able to sit in meditation with my inner father. I feel his presence in the fluttering leaves of a tall oak and sense his newfound freedom.

Letter to Mom

Thầy has given everyone an assignment to complete by New Year's. We create lists of our positive and negative qualities. Thầy requests that we make the list of positives longer than the list of negatives. After completing the lists, we study each quality to see if we can discern its origin. I see that a majority of the characteristics on both of my lists were present in my dad. I'm not surprised. He was my primary male role model. Some of my qualities come from Mom. Shortly before Father died, I thanked him for the many ways he contributed to our family. Mom was in the room, but it hadn't occurred to me at the time to thank her too. Now, from Plum Village, I write to thank her for all the good traits she has bequeathed me. When I call a couple of weeks later, she tells me that when she read the letter, she cried. She asks me to thank my teacher. She wishes she'd written a letter like that to her own mother. I tell her she still can. I've stumbled upon a beautiful way to share my practice with Mom.

Reflection—Impermanence

Buddhism posits that there are three characteristics common throughout everything in life. Known as the "three marks of existence," they are ill-being, nonself, and impermanence. "Because of impermanence," Thầy tells us, "*everything* is possible."

I see my own part of *everything* as affected, if not determined, by conditions, external and internal. External conditions include people, places, and things I've been in direct contact with, along with society, the global village, and our Mother Earth. The term *internal conditions* refers to the seeds in my store consciousness. Those receiving water become robust, whether they're wholesome, unwholesome, or neutral seeds, and they determine internal responses that translate into thoughts, words, and actions.

With mindfulness I can bring more awareness to how I respond to conditions, as I learned in therapy with Rudy. In the presence of ingrained habits, it can take extraordinary conditions to bring about transformation. We three men in grief, as recounted in the vignette Brothers, were able to affect each other and our future choices. But, as I recount in the vignette Dying, sometimes conditions find us, and we can only endeavor to be present for them. Regardless, all these conditions continually affect us, and therefore, they are not just in the past but are deeply present here and now.

Nourishing our own well-being begins with cultivating awareness of the kinds of nutriments we consume. We're constantly receiving sense impressions that enter our store consciousness. With attention we can become more aware of both sensory input and our positive and negative reactions to it from our body-heart-mind. In Plum Village, becoming aware of a fresh energetic connection, I introduced myself to Nel. At home, I refrained from responding unskillfully to my dad's Alzheimer's behavior. These are choices we can make. Becoming more aware of the effects food and drink had on my body, I stopped drinking coffee because of its impact on my nervous system. Profound changes in my volition occurred as I discovered teaching to be my vocation. After experiencing a life-changing resonance with Thầy and his teachings, I dedicated myself to his path and to sharing it with others.

In my own development, promoting healthy thoughts and reducing unhealthy ones—practicing with the nutriment of consciousness—has been most challenging. Some seeds in the store consciousness inherited from my ancestors were negative. One of them was denial. Fortunately, all seeds are impermanent. They're continually modified by each successive generation in response to fresh causes and conditions. But it takes work to feel and identify them, to remember they are not actually ours individually, that we have choices in our actions, even if an ancestral seed is drawing us toward an ingrained response. In my case, I also have a propensity toward spiritual practice. I have been drawn in this life toward mindfulness and transformation. These seeds can embrace the darker seeds of fear and oppression watered in my ancestors and allow new and ever-changing forms to emerge. I am grateful to Thầy for showing me the way, and I do my best to practice what I've learned, and thus in my own humble way to be one of the many streams of his continuation.

Invitation

Sit in a comfortable position. Relax. Let your eyes close and breathe
in and out slowly three times. Invite your life into your awareness,
and notice whatever feelings or thoughts related to impermanence
come to mind. Stay present with them. When you feel ready, open
your eyes.

PART FOUR

INTERBEING

If you are a poet, you will see that there is a cloud floating in this sheet of paper. Without a cloud, there will be no rain; without rain, the trees cannot grow; and without trees, we cannot make paper. The cloud is essential for the paper to exist. If the cloud is not here, the sheet of paper cannot be here either. So, we can say that the cloud and the paper inter-are. "Interbeing" is a word that is not in the dictionary yet, but if we combine the prefix "inter-" with the verb "to be," we have a new verb, inter-be.

If we look into this sheet of paper even more deeply, we can see the sunshine in it. If the sunshine is not there, the forest cannot grow. In fact, nothing can grow. Even we cannot grow without sunshine. And so, we know the sunshine is also in this sheet of paper. The paper and the sunshine inter-are. And if we continue to look, we can see the logger who cut the tree and brought it to the mill to be transformed into paper. And we see the wheat. We know the logger cannot exist without his daily bread, and therefore the wheat that became his bread is also in this sheet of paper. And the logger's father and mother are in it too. When we look in this way, we see that without all these things, this sheet of paper cannot exist.

Looking even more deeply, we can see we are in it too. This is not difficult to see, because when you look at a sheet of paper, the sheet of paper is part of our perception. Your mind is in here and mine is also. So, we can say that everything is in here with this sheet of paper. You cannot point out one thing that is not here—time, space, the earth, the rain, the minerals in the soil, the sunshine, the cloud, the river, the heat. Everything co-exists with this sheet of paper. That is why I think the word inter-be should be in the dictionary. "To be" is to inter-be. You cannot just be by yourself alone. You have to inter-be with every other thing. This sheet of paper is, because everything else is.

—Thich Nhat Hanh, *The Heart of Understanding*

This teaching invites us to look deeply into ourselves to better understand the elements that continually come together to form "us." Intellectually we know that we're born with the genetic structure of our ancestors, and since birth we've "ingested" the four nutriments— food, sense impressions, volition, and consciousness— all formed from a myriad of other sources. Yet we continue to see ourselves as a non-changing, separate, independent self. According to Buddhist psychology, this illusion is the work of *manas*, a layer of consciousness between store consciousness and mind consciousness.

Before Dharma talks, we sometimes chant *Namo Avalokiteshvara*, the name of the bodhisattva of compassion, to help us water our seed of connection. Doing so, we offer compassion first to ourselves, then to a loved one, and then to all suffering beings, much like *metta* meditation in the *vipassana* school of Buddhism. Suffering, like happiness, has no ownership. It is universal. Deep listening during Dharma sharing, Dharma talks, ceremonies, or in the context of any relationship also offers opportunities to let go of one's mental self and connect with others from the heart. In the ultimate dimension, we may find that the suffering of the world reflects our own suffering, just as our suffering reflects that of the world. And this is equally true of joy and happiness.

However, many of us have a deeply ingrained worldview given at birth. Letting go of our illusion of being a permanent, separate self may take place over time, with energetic practice. Once we're able to look deeply at clouds, waves, flowers, or pieces of paper and truly see them as everchanging physical formations without a separate existence, we may be ready to contemplate our own identity and, following Thây's advice, ask ourselves *"Are you sure?"* about whatever seems true.

Continuing to look with an attitude of curiosity, we pay attention to and *accept* the evidence we observe rather than ignore or dismiss it. We shift from our usual historical-dimension perspective to seeing ultimate reality, the *suchness* or true nature of life. This is not a rational process or one we can control. Uprooting years of habitual thinking and "understanding" is a long-term venture. Rather than giving up on this aspiration when nothing seems to be changing, we can cease striving and entrust it to the seed of awakening in our store consciousness, to our Buddha nature.

Chapter 7

MUD

*Most people are afraid of suffering. But suffering is a
kind of mud to help the lotus flower of happiness grow.
There can be no lotus flower without the mud.*

–Thich Nhat Hanh, *No Mud, No Lotus*

The Holocaust

From my winter experience in Plum Village, I bring home a new
friendship with Gabriela, a therapist from Hamburg, my father's
hometown. When we meet, she's interested to learn I live outside of
Washington, DC. "Have you visited the Holocaust Museum there?"
she asks. The United States Holocaust Memorial Museum has
recently opened, but I haven't yet felt prepared for that emotional
shock. Gabriela tells me that her father, a Nazi soldier during World
War II, was captured by the Allies and interned in a prisoner-of-war
camp in South Carolina. As he refuses to speak to her about those
times, Gabriela has decided to travel to the US to visit the site of that
camp and the new museum. "Please stay with us when you come to
DC," I say. "We can visit the museum together."

Several months later as we enter the door of the museum, Gabriela and I receive identification cards. Each card describes the life
before, during, and (for survivors) after the war of a "companion"

who will accompany us on our tour. Gabriela and I, first-generation descendants of opposing sides of the war, walk silently together, holding hands. Through simple presence, we take in one exhibit after another. Some exhibits tell stories in words, others in pictures, and one with a display of thousands of shoes of the dead, piled up like corpses. I could never have done this alone. Gabriela's companionship is a blessing. We don't speak. My ancestral suffering has come to the fore. With the blessing of this new friendship, I begin to grieve it.

Richie

Fast forward to 1996. I'm in Plum Village again, this time for two weeks in the summer. I stay in touch with Elisabeth through letters and occasional phone calls. Life at home has been warm hugs one minute and tension the next. How refreshing it is to dwell in a stable environment!

Toward the end of my stay, I'm unsettled by furnishing changes Elisabeth tells me she's making at home. As my spacious world closes in, I reach out to share this with Sr. Jina, a wise nun, who has become a friend. After listening quietly, she replies, "Richard, what I really hear you say is that you're troubled because Elisabeth is not giving you the love you need." I've shared nothing of the kind, but this is just how I feel. I nod.

She continues, "But, Richard, there is only one person who knows the love you need and can give it to you, and that is you. And if you give yourself the love you need, you'll be able to accept with gratitude whatever Elisabeth has to offer." Her words strike deep.

"The one who needs to be loved," she continues, "is not this Richard. Little five-year-old Richard is longing to be loved. How were you called as a child?"

"I was Richie then," I reply. "But what can I do now to give Richie the love he needed then?"

"First, when you sit, see yourself as the Great Mother and hold little Richie in your Great Mother lap. As you meditate, shower him with all the love he needs. After several weeks of this practice, inhabit little Richie sitting on the Great Mother's lap and receive all her love."

I know exactly what love is needed, and I begin right away. Wondrously satisfied to enfold my needy five-year-old with love, I hold him in my arms and feel tenderness and affection flow from my heart into his.

When it comes time to become the child and receive this love, I find it impossible. I cannot feel the Great Mother's embrace. I try several times, always with the same result. I give up and go back to my regular meditation practice.

Five years later, in 2001 during a twenty-one-day retreat at Plum Village, I'm riddled with negativity and self-doubt. My friend Eveline, whom I'd discovered was my partner in the hands' practice in 1992, comes to my aid. We're sitting on a ridge, looking out over the vineyards and a setting sun; Eveline begins to describe a meditation in which she felt her life swirl around her like a cyclone as she sat in its eye, its calm center, just to watch and breathe.

"Would you like to try this, Richard?" she asks.

I nod.

"Place an open palm on the ground," Eveline advises, then she gently places her hand on top of mine to help me stay grounded and centered.

As my life events arise and swirl about me, I see recent discomfort, then pain from years earlier. Suffering spins around me, interwoven with other moments, some touchingly beautiful. After breathing and smiling to the whole of my life, I open my eyes to a new sense of calm. During this visualization, I was not caught by these emotions. I was simply present with them.

Returning home, I find myself repeatedly in the grips of a dark emotional cyclone. At times I remember to find my way to that calm center. The center brings relief, but only briefly. Then, unexpectedly, I discover Leslie Rawls's *Mindfulness Bell* article about transforming her grief at the time of her father's death. Leslie describes her mourning as a whirlwind, her innocent little girl caught up in the storm. She tries again and again without success to bring her little girl down. Finally, she understands that she must embrace the whole whirlwind, little girl and all. I realize, thanks to Leslie, that when I sat in the eye of my own cyclone, I created a separation between myself and the swirl of my emotions. I was temporarily calm but not transformed.

As I meditate the following morning, alone in our loft, Sr. Jina's self-loving practice comes back to me. Suddenly I see that in being the child cradled in the lap of the Great Mother, my goal was only to receive. I never really plumbed the depths of Richie's fears and neediness. This time I climb into my child's skin—terrors, longing, and all—and for the first time, I feel love's big embrace.

Causes and Conditions

Another lesson arrives the week after Christmas in 1998, during my first visit to Green Mountain Dharma Center, then Thầy's temple in Vermont. When I arrive, I'm tired and unhappy. The past year has been a challenge at home and at school. After three days in the quiet, snow-covered hills of Vermont, I'm relaxed and smiling. My sole concern is to take this peace home with me. Hoping for advice and reassurance, I ask Sister Annabel, the abbess of the center, for a consultation. Sr. Annabel, educated at London University in classical languages, became the first Westerner to be ordained as a monastic by Thầy in 1988. I begin by describing my return home from previous retreats: "When I get home, I'm walking on air, Sister Annabel, but I'm like a tire with a slow leak. Friends meeting me a week or so after my return don't know I've been anywhere."

Sister Annabel laughs. Then looking me in the eye she says, "Richard, you know this practice is the practice of the present moment. The Maryland present moment is different from the Vermont present moment. You are present in both places, but all the other causes and conditions are different. Don't expect to bring Vermont back to Maryland."

She pauses, giving me time to feel my sadness and resignation, then continues: "Here's the good news: The causes and conditions in Maryland are perfect for the practice that needs to be done there."

But what exactly *is* the practice that needs to be done in Maryland?

Expanding mindfulness from my meditation cushion to the rest of life is an ongoing task. I need to practice better communication. My longstanding habits of judgment and defensiveness are patently unmindful. During one tumultuous time, I bring this up with my friend Anh-Huong. "When you're communicating," she advises, "notice who is doing the communicating. Is it the sixty-four-year-old or the five-year-old?" Her advice is a gold mine. My five-year-old is the needy me who easily feels invisible and uncared for. He crops up when communications are strained. But he's also there at times when I'm alone and feeling anxious, sad, upset, or other bleak emotions. When I awaken in the morning feeling down and needing to befriend myself, it's my five-year-old who wants comfort.

Therapy

After meeting Thich Nhat Hanh in 1989, I decide to limit myself to therapists with an appreciation of Eastern practice. This decision stems from Thầy's orientation toward well-being. He teaches that sources of distress are as much a part of us as sources of health. I need not remove the suffering parts of me but embrace them tenderly. With acceptance and understanding, I can heal and transform them. Furthermore, wellness has as much to do with strengthening the best in me as it does with transforming the worst. This is Rudy's approach. It is Thầy's approach. Both have proved immeasurably helpful.

I met Ted Cmarada at my first retreat with Thầy in 1989. Ted is a therapist in Frederick, Maryland, about an hour's drive from Takoma Park, where I live. He is also a mindfulness practitioner and leader of a Sangha. I told Ted then that I wished he lived closer. Over the next nine years I worked with a variety of therapists. Each was helpful at the time, but I'm aware of no significant transformation. In 1999, I begin seeing Ted. Leaving DC after school and driving into the Maryland countryside turns out to be great preparation for our visits.

I arrive at Ted's office and unburden myself. Ted responds with helpful wisdom, often a lesson in the Dharma that makes good sense. But this wisdom is not so easy to put into practice. "Richard," Ted says, "you're working too hard on yourself." I've received this teaching time and again. Ted does his best to help me understand Suzuki Roshi's observation, "Each of you is perfect the way you are ... and you can use a little improvement."[25] How much easier to sprout from the soil of self-acceptance!

Ted and Thầy water the seeds in me that later produce my lamp transmission poem, "This Freedom," which appears in the Prologue. Self-acceptance grows slowly in tandem with self-compassion. I also begin to feel more balance with and compassion for the suffering that underlies Elisabeth's behavior. Even when her words say otherwise, I still sense her compassion for me. We are definitely a work in progress.

I continue to practice with the suffering of my five-year-old. In a letter to Therese in 2001, I write:

> I awoke at 3:00 a.m. and, unable to sleep, I began to meditate. A tightness grabbed my chest. I repeatedly used the five steps (breathe, relax, feel, watch, allow) I'd just read about in Stephen Cope's book Yoga and the Quest for the True Self. My feelings intensified. I felt the distance between my dad and me, his rigidity vis-à-vis proper conduct and appearance, his disappointment when I didn't meet his expectations, my loneliness and fear at those times. As the distance became greater,

suddenly I intuited my dad's loneliness, his entrapment in the role his own father had played in his life. For several minutes, I wept. Then the crying passed, and I went back to bed. This was big for me. My personal practice now centers on staying present with a residue of childhood tension that seems ever-present. I hope to ride these waves again and again until they are my friends.

Lesson from Shoshanna

Shoshanna is the vehicle for one of my greatest lessons in equanimity. When she's thirteen, I go on retreat to Deer Park, Thầy's monastery in Escondido, California; I borrow our family's single cell phone. Arriving at Deer Park, I call our landline to let Elisabeth know I've arrived, but unfamiliar with the phone, I mistakenly listen to a message that had been left for Shoshanna by a friend. The friend tells Shoshanna that she should confess her responsibility for some unnamed thing Elisabeth and I have blamed on this friend. I have no idea what the friend is talking about and am quite upset. Fortunately, my friend Peggy Rowe is also on retreat at Deer Park. Peggy helps me let go of my suffering for a moment by asking me to reflect on the kind of relationship I want to have with Shoshanna. I cool down and step back. On arriving home, I invite Shoshanna to have a private conversation. Handing her the phone, I apologize for inadvertently listening to a message intended for her, then invite her to listen to it.

"Would you like to tell me anything about this message?" I ask.

"No," Shoshanna replies.

"I'd welcome hearing about it from you any time you do have something you want to share," I say. Then I let it go. I'm glad I've learned to ask for help. Peggy helped me let go of separation and feel connection. Without her, I'm afraid to think of what might have taken place that night.

Letter to Mom and Dad

In 2013, eight years after my mother's death and nineteen after my father's, I write them a letter. I've already thanked each of them for bequeathing me their positive traits, but I've voiced nothing about the negatives. "It's not helpful to dwell on the negative," my mother would say. But to neglect the negative would be a disservice to me and my family. So, I write to say that over the last nineteen years I've begun to see the negative traits we share: my mom's busy mind, my dad's judgment. I'm more than aware—I feel regret and some-times blame. I'm sure these traits have been present in our DNA for generations. Whether our ancestors were aware of them or not, their unwholesome traits led to suffering, while their positive qual-ities enriched their own lives and ours. I've been granted a great gift—a mindfulness practice I can devote myself to, on behalf of all my ancestors and descendants. With mindfulness, I'm more aware and appreciative of the positive traits I've received, and with mind-fulness I've begun to transform the negatives. I do this on behalf of all our family.

Thầy sometimes refers to the "goodness of suffering." He points out how, without suffering, we cannot truly appreciate happiness, and, equally important, we don't develop compassion. I don't doubt that my parents felt compassion for Bob, even though it wasn't openly expressed. They were deeply caring people. But they never seemed in touch with their own suffering or with self-compassion. This helps me understand why their happiness was tempered, as well.

Chapter 8

GROWING FLOWERS

Happiness is not an individual matter.

—Thich Nhat Hanh,
At Home in the World

Flower Watering

Members of communities need to stay up to date with each other for happiness to flourish. To this end, practitioners in the Plum Village tradition perform a four-part ceremony called "Beginning Anew." Everyone sits in a circle facing each other. In the first part, after bowing to the community and retrieving a flower from the middle of the circle, a member "waters the flowers" of another member by expressing gratitude for the particular contributions of their actions or their way of being. Time is given after each flower is watered for the recipient to fully receive what has been shared. All four parts are described by Brother Bao Tang on the Plum Village website as follows:

FLOWER WATERING

This is a chance to share our appreciation for the other person. We may mention specific instances that the other person said or did something that we had admired. This is an opportunity to shine light on the other's strengths and contributions to the Sangha and to encourage the growth of his or her positive qualities.

SHARING REGRETS

We may mention any unskillfulness in our actions, speech or thoughts that we have not yet had an opportunity to apologize for.

EXPRESSING A HURT

We may share how we felt hurt by an interaction with another practitioner, due to his or her actions, speech or thoughts. (Before expressing a hurt, it's best to water the other person's flower first by sharing two positive qualities we have observed in him or her. Expressing a hurt may be best performed one-on-one with another practitioner rather than in a group setting. You can ask for a third party you both trust and respect to be present, if desired.)

SHARING A LONG-TERM DIFFICULTY & ASKING FOR SUPPORT

At times we each have difficulties and pain arise from our past that surface in the present. When we share an issue that we are dealing with, we allow people around us to understand us better and offer the support we really need.[26]

During short retreats, these ceremonies may consist only of flower watering. However, in the community setting, practicing all four parts can be very important. Bhante, a large German monk from a different tradition, who has come to sojourn at Plum Village for several weeks, often shares the Dharma with all within earshot. Initially, I'm attracted by his intelligence and his teaching. However, soon I realize it's interfering with my personal practice, and I begin to avoid him. On the day of a Beginning Anew ceremony, a friend confides in me that he might feel called upon to express his upset with Bhante's behavior this evening. As the ceremony's flower watering draws to a close, I begin to feel my friend's tension in my own stomach. Suddenly, Bhante bows, walks to the center of our circle and clasps the flower. Returning to his cushion, he bows to all of us and clears his throat and begins to talk in his deep voice: "If some of you are having problems with my unskillful speech, I apologize. I invite you to talk with me directly. In my tradition, retreats are completely silent, so speech is never an issue for me."

When we end, I approach Bhante and ask to get together the next day after breakfast. We eat together, sitting across from each other. After washing our dishes, we begin to speak. I thank Bhante for his apology and let him know that I feel complete. I ask him where he comes from in Germany. When I tell him that my father was a Jewish refugee from Hamburg, Bhante initiates a conversation about the Holocaust, which continues to deeply trouble him. We part with a mutual understanding and warm feeling for each other. Beginning Anew has done its work.

Smiling

It's no accident that the word *smile* appears so often in this book. Smiling is one of the core practices Thich Nhat Hanh teaches. For those who have difficulty smiling, Thầy suggests a half-smile. He refers to smiling as "mouth yoga." In Plum Village we become aware of the joy of doing walking meditation with the Sangha and smile. We smile as we eat delicious Vietnamese meals. We smile as we see others smiling—others who may well have been Vietnamese boat people who suffered terribly during the American War and its aftermath.

Some gathas remind us to smile in order to nurture our own happiness. Here is one I often recite on awakening:

Waking up this morning, I smile.
Twenty-four brand new hours are before me.

I vow to live fully in each moment
and to look at all beings with eyes of compassion.[27]

During total relaxation practice, as we scan our bodies, we can say
to ourselves:

Breathing in, I'm aware of my heart.
Breathing out, I smile to my heart.

A gatha I write during the 1992 twenty-one-day retreat reminds me
to connect Sr. Jina's smile to my own:

Your smile is like a bell of mindfulness.
When I see it, I touch my own inner joy.

But is happiness always available? In a question-and-answer
session with Thầy, Joan Halifax asks if it's okay for the terminally ill
patients she accompanies to say "present moment, only moment"
instead of "present moment, wonderful moment."

"No," replies Thầy. "Wonder can be found in every moment—
in the blue sky, the feeling of the air on our skin, the miracle of life
itself."

Wonder is also available to me. But I'm not always happy. Sometimes I need to focus on unpleasant things that I or others have done
or neglected to do. Sometimes I choose to focus on such things even
when I don't need to. These choices are made unconsciously, out of
habit. When I become aware that I'm going down such a road, I can
choose a different path. To make this choice, I must first be aware
that my mind is engaging in "gratuitous negativity." Then I have to be
aware that this is a choice, and I can make a different one. Sometimes
I get to make this new choice repeatedly. Doing so isn't easy for me,
and I'm far from consistent. This is how I try to take responsibility
for my own happiness. It reminds me of a quote of Goethe's I heard

from one of my friends: "Let everyone sweep in front of his own door, and the whole world will be clean."

Celebration

When asked about what he taught, the Buddha routinely replied, "Suffering and the end of suffering." The fifth and sixth of the sixteen practices outlined in his Ānāpānasati Sutta (Discourse on the Full Awareness of Breathing) are

> 'Breathing in, I feel joyful.
> Breathing out, I feel joyful.'
> He or she practices like this.
> 'Breathing in, I feel happy.
> Breathing out, I feel happy.'
> He or she practices like this.[28]

Yet I find Thầy's stress on watering positive seeds unusual among Buddhist teachers and practice centers in the West. Nowhere in Plum Village are joy and happiness emphasized more than in the many celebrations and songs. Long retreats always include at least one large celebration, whether it's a full moon ritual, a Rose Ceremony honoring parents, or a three-day Tết Lunisolar New Year's celebration.

These celebrations often include festive Vietnamese food, elaborate costumes and decorations, and performances by practitioners—often musical or comedic in nature. Not all celebrations are elaborate. At the beginning of one of Thầy's Dharma talks in the summer of 1993, he invites a child to stand next to him and announce that today we will celebrate "Today's Day." Thầy suggests we start every day with this celebration.

Informal tea ceremonies, also called "be-ins," often conclude retreats in the Plum Village tradition and also are found in Sangha gatherings. Usually announced in advance, participants read poems—sometimes old favorites, sometimes just written by them—sing, play music, tell stories, and participate in skits with others from their country or their Dharma-sharing family. In one never-to-be-forgotten Plum Village skit in 2004, our Dharma-sharing family performed the "Wizard of Is" with Phap Huu, now abbot of Upper Hamlet, then a teenage novice, playing the role of the Wizard—Thầy.

Once in Plum Village, I organize a small, informal celebration. After I discover that my new friend Susanne is a jazz pianist who has just completed a CD and has an advance copy with her, I hatch a plan. My roommates—Marius from the Netherlands, Salvo from Sicily, and Dene from England—are all jazz aficionados, so I purchase a large amount of dark chocolate and invite a few friends to come to our room on the last night of the twenty-one-day retreat. As we become intoxicated on chocolate and listen to Susanne's CD, Marius makes four copies of it on his computer using blank CDs intended for Thầy's Dharma talks (with permission of the monastics), and the next morning, I return Susanne's master CD along with payment for four copies. She's thrilled to meet the audience for her recording.

Monastics have their own celebrations. They visit each other's rooms during the three-day Têt celebration, bringing goodies and musical instruments to accompany singing. I'm fortunate to be able to join a different kind of monastic celebration. One year, when teaching commitments delay my arrival for a twenty-one-day retreat, I arrange to stay a week after the retreat concludes. On the final day of the retreat, I bid farewell to friends old and new, and in the evening I'm bereft with loneliness. The next morning, I walk down to the Lower Hamlet seeking connection. Happily for me, Sr. Jina is available. After listening deeply to my woes, she corrects me. "You say that all your friends have left Upper Hamlet, but that's not true." After a short pause, she concludes, "You're still there." Indeed, I'm still there, and am I not one of my friends? I begin to lighten up. The following day turns out to be the most joyful of my stay. Monastics have rented canoes and invite me to join them for a day paddling on the Dordogne

River, but not just paddling. There are songs and splashing as we look up at medieval castles perched high above the riverbanks—a perfect way for me to feel a part of something bigger than my loneliness.

Song

Songs play an important role in mindfulness retreats in the Plum Village tradition. As we enter the meditation hall and find our cushions or chairs, a monastic often leads us in practice songs, many of which support happiness:

HAPPINESS IS HERE AND NOW

Happiness is here and now
 I have dropped my worries.
Nowhere to go, nothing to do,
No longer in a hurry.

Happiness is here and now
I have dropped my worries.
Somewhere to go, something to do,
Still not in a hurry.[29]

During retreats we also sing practice songs before commencing walking meditation and sometimes at the beginning or end of working meditation. Back in Washington, singing is a popular way of concluding our Sangha sittings. These songs become part of me, and I often sing them to myself as well, brightening my day.

Hugging

Soon after he began teaching in the West, Thầy developed hugging meditation, for me one of the most profound Plum Village happiness practices. In Vietnam, public hugging is not a part of the culture, but in the West people asked Thầy for hugs. Dismayed by the perfunctory nature of many of the hugs he witnessed—just a second or two and a slap on the back, Thầy developed the practice of mindful hugging.

Two people look each other in the eye and bow deeply in recognition of the other's Buddha nature, the other's capacity for enlightenment. Then the two embrace and breathe together three times—aware of bringing their full presence during the first breath, aware of the the other's presence during the second, and aware that this present moment will never come 'round again during the third. Then they separate mindfully, and, looking at each other once again, bow deeply. Hugging meditation ensues whenever one practitioner's invitation is accepted by another. I most often engage in this practice when I meet or leave old Dharma friends and when I join the wholesale hugging of newly ordained participants at the conclusion of transmission ceremonies.

In 1996 I enjoy two weeks of Plum Village's summer retreat at the recently opened New Hamlet. Located near Thầy's hermitage, it's a half-hour drive from the rest of Plum Village. Because of the proximity to his primary dwelling, it's not uncommon for Thầy to join the community for meditation and meals. One bright morning as I walk into the library, Thầy enters the opposite door. He's almost always accompanied by an attendant, but this morning he's alone, and he's heading in my direction to leave by the door I've just entered. I smile, breathe deeply, bow—then say, "Your teaching has benefited me so much, Thầy. Would it be okay to do hugging meditation?" He nods. We bow. The longest three breaths of my life follow as we hug. We part, bow again, and Thầy departs. I return to my room, lie on my bed, and sob.

The Mind of Love

In 1996 Parallax Press publishes Thầy's Dharma talks from my first Plum Village retreat in the book *Cultivating the Mind of Love*. As I read it, I'm back in Plum Village seeing the young nun stir Thầy's heart and ultimately help him deepen his commitment to touch the deepest level of his being—his *bodhicitta*, his awakened nature, which Thầy calls the *mind of love*. This powerful energy infuses his life. I feel it in Thầy's presence and in the Dharma he transmits. I feel it in Plum Village, in the smiles, the songs, the hugs, the celebrations, in my friendships, in my Dharma-sharing group, and in the Sangha as a whole. There I begin to touch it in myself.

Chapter 9

RETURN AGAIN

Return again, return again.
Return to the land of your soul.
Return to who you are.
Return to what you are.
Return to where you are,
born and reborn again[30]

—Rabbi Shlomo Carlebach,
"Return Again"

When we respect our blood ancestors and our spiritual ancestors, we feel rooted. If we find ways to cherish and develop our spiritual heritage, we will avoid the kind of alienation that is destroying society, and we will become whole again. … Learning to touch deeply the jewels of our own tradition will allow us to understand and appreciate the values of other traditions, and this will benefit everyone.

—Thich Nhat Hanh,
Living Buddha, Living Christ

Ancestral Home

In the early 1990s, Thich Nhat Hanh begins to talk about the importance of *not* cutting ourselves off from our spiritual roots. It's through these roots, he tells us, that the spiritual energy of our ancestors can be tapped. All I need do to understand this is look at the portrait taken by my uncle of Jacob Sonderling, the rabbi of the Reform synagogue in Hamburg which my great grandfather Amandus attended with my young father Rudi.

Rabbi Sonderling's chiseled visage is that of a holy man. Growing up, I knew no Jew remotely like him. Now I've found Thich Nhat Hanh and accepted his invitation to enter a different one of the 84,000 Dharma doors to enlightenment.

Rabbi Jacob Sonderling
PHOTO BY HANS BRADY

In 1996, I begin to practice the ceremony called Touching the Earth [Appendix 3] that Thây has recently introduced. The rite consists of three prostrations. The first is a body prayer that connects me to all my spiritual and blood ancestors and descendants. The second connects me to all people and species alive at this moment. And the third invites me to transcend my view of having a separate existence limited in space and time.

One spring morning in 1997 as I practice this body prayer, I receive a vision of an old woman—a great grandchild of mine—pointing to a picture of me in an ancient photo album and saying to her granddaughter, "This was your great-great-great-grandfather Richard. He was the last Jewish member of the family, but we don't know much about that." I know from my experience at B'nai Or that my Jewish seed is alive, but I've given Shoshanna no access to this part of her heritage—not that I want her to become a practicing Jew, but I do want her to know more of me and more of this part of herself. For that to happen, my Judaism needs to be available, especially to me. I must water my roots.

My friend Esther suggests I meet Reb Zalman Schachter-Shalomi, a contemporary Jewish holy man, spiritual father of the Jewish Renewal movement, and founder of B'nai Or. Hoping to study with Reb Zalman, I decide to explore Judaism for a week at Elat Chayyim, a Jewish Renewal center in the Catskill Mountains in upstate New York. The first evening we gather under a large canopy in the field where we are welcomed. We're invited to introduce ourselves and be introduced to the teachers. We rise, identifying through Jewish affiliation and in other ways. I'm pleased to see that three-fourths of us practice meditation but disappointed to learn that Reb Zalman cannot be present at the retreat. I enroll in Rabbi Miles Krassen's class on meditation. I'm also interested in Neila Carlebach's class on angels after she tells the story of herself at age three, falling unnoticed into a construction pit. Helpless, she is left in the dark pit for the night, her cries unheard. Later she is pulled out by a silent, mysterious stranger.

Lessons

In the past I approached Buddhist retreats hoping to find something of value but having no clue what it might be. Those experiences were always rich and surprising, but even during longer retreats I took few notes and did little journaling. On plane trips home from Plum Village, I wrote in my journal—capturing people, events, and teachings I wanted to remember. But these were not the *most* nourishing fruit. With the nonverbal energy-transmissions I received from Thầy and the Sangha, I came home a changed person. Elat Chayyim is different. Here almost everything is new for me. Wanting to understand, I take copious notes, but there is little in my memory of Judaism for my experience here to connect with.

Miles' first class moves slowly between a Hebrew text and his English translation—passages that describe the need for a meditation practice to develop a sense of God's awesomeness and to develop our love. We engage in a meditation holding this intention. First we visualize and then trace the awesome light of God back to its source. After practicing this with people, animals, trees, mountains, and ourselves, we imagine these same beams of light emanating back to us from their source. We're invited to understand the fear in the first part of the meditation as the energy that fuels our practice. The second part focuses on devotion. Deeply moved, I see my father become transparent, move back to the source, then return as light. Is this what I've come for?

I'm ready to trust my intuition that Neila's course on angels will also be right. A short talk with her confirms this. I enroll in two courses on Jewish mysticism with teachers whose lives embody it. The numinous aspect of religion, so absent from my youth, is what attracted me to the spiritual practice of Quakers. Now, newly steeped in the Jewish mystery tradition, I find a second home.

While I don't usually see angels, I'm struck by Neila's presence. Because I lack biblical background, I grasp only a fraction of her teachings. However, something quite unexpected happens when she brings a crystal to class and offers to "read" our colors by watching it swing on a chain over our opened palms. She tells me my color is green, the color associated with the heart. The next day she explains that each person has a particular Hebrew letter. Using the crystal again, she finds each of our letters. Mine is *mem* (מ), the letter associated with water. I'm amazed. When I received the Five Precepts eight years before, Thich Nhat Hanh gave me the lineage name *Clear Water of the Heart*. Until now I never really identified with that name. Now it circles back in a fresh way. Water is related to transformation. It makes sense. On both paths, my task seems to be heart-opening transformation.

I also attend a morning prayer service with Jay, a new friend. Standing and chanting with others, I feel my father's presence beside me three years after his passing. In a loving gesture at just that moment, Jay slips his *tallit* or prayer shawl over my shoulders. Tears stream down my face. Several days later, the morning Shabbat service led by Rabbi Shefa Gold is punctuated by joyful chants urging us to our feet to dance. I'm in an altered state. At the end I confide to a young rabbi, another member of Neila's class, "I haven't had an experience like this since my last Grateful Dead concert!" "Neither have I," he replies.

Western Buddhism

Soon after returning home, I meet Steve Marcus at Seekers Church, a progressive Christian church in Washington, DC that Elisabeth and Shoshanna are attending. Steve's partner, Jeanne, is a member there. Steve has a strong background in Judaism and is interested in learning about Elat Chayyim. He accompanies me there two years later in the summer of 1999. This time I have the opportunity to take a course on the *siddur*, the Jewish prayer book, from Reb Zalman. I'm able to understand some of his teachings, but, more importantly, like Thây, Reb Zalman transmits an ineffable energy of love and awakening.

Toward the end of the week, I sit in a short consultation with the Rebbe. When I tell him I'm a student of Thầy, his eyes light up. He expresses his tremendous admiration for Thầy's teachings, then goes on to share his concern about what he sees happening with Buddhism in the West. "People are trading in their rich spiritual traditions—their rituals marking life transitions and celebrations of the seasons—for sitting on a cushion. This won't provide enough nourishment to the next generation." Having not grown up with a rich Jewish practice, I've found Plum Village practice very nourishing, but I understand what Reb Zalman is saying.

When I leave Elat Chayyim, I travel north to Green Mountain Monastery, Thầy's temple in South Woodstock, Vermont. Having a few days before Thầy will arrive to lead a retreat, I share Reb Zalman's concern with Sister Annabel. There's merit in the Rabbi's apprehension, she responds, but he overlooks an important historical fact. Whenever Buddhism has been brought into new parts of the world, it's been assimilated into the local religion and culture within several hundred years. "In time, we'll have a Judeo-Christian Buddhism in the West."

I feel glad I've been led to experience Buddhism and Judaism independently. Western and Jewish though I am, I experience the Plum Village tradition as my path. At Elat Chayyim, even as I drew closer to my ancestors than ever before, this becomes clear.

Back home, I want to continue Jewish studies, but how? I think of Steve. Maybe I can study Judaism with him. Steve likes the idea and proposes that we become *hevruta*, study partners, rather than teacher and student. On Friday mornings, Steve begins coming to our home for breakfast followed by a study session. He suggests several books written by contemporary Jews with a contemplative bent or ones from mystical Hassidic Judaism. Together we select the next book to read and discuss. Here is the Jewish education I missed growing up. Our study sessions end only when we move to Vermont in 2008. They have been an irreplaceable treasure.

Reflection—Interbeing

Interbeing, a reality of the ultimate dimension Thây often shares in his teaching, should not be confused with *interdependence*. In the historical dimension, separate entities can be interdependent. In the ultimate dimension, separate entities do not exist. Looking deeply in the ultimate dimension at anything, we might see that it contains the entire cosmos. Looking at myself, I see the present moment taking up residence in my store consciousness. As the present is a continuation of the past, the past is in me, too. Thây would say "Richard is made of non-Richard elements." This multitude includes my grandfather Amandus, the Holocaust, and my five-year-old self.

Interbeing is ubiquitous. Thây talks about the interbeing of happiness and suffering. Without suffering, happiness lacks a basis for existence. We are happy with our non-toothache only after experiencing recovery from a toothache. Happiness coexists with suffering. In my experience of depression, although its seed was strong, seeds of wellbeing present in my store consciousness, once watered, were also ready to sprout. Thây also reminds us that suffering is a necessary condition for learning self-compassion and compassion for others. This is the basis of compassion practice, wishing that all beings be free from suffering, and *metta* practice, wishing happiness for all beings. Suffering is not only a potential source of happiness. It can also be a result. If happiness isn't nurtured or if it's clung to, suffering is a likely outcome.

Religions also inter-are. Thây often mentions that Buddhism is made of non-Buddhist elements—an observation echoed by Sister Annabel. After I returned from Elat Chayyim, I realized I had gone there with a question: Was Judaism my true path? Was it not only the religion of my ancestors but also a path with the God I didn't find in Buddhism? The response I found came from my heart. It was not in the words but in the emotions and the energy beneath them. The suffering and the joy we shared at Elat Chayyim were universal.

They were also present at Plum Village, acknowledged and cared for in both places where they lit the way to the Ultimate and to God. The two paths differed in their histories, practices, and world views. Buddhism had given me a pair of glasses through which I could look deeply and see what seemed to be the heart of Judaism. What I was discovering was already in me.

Invitation

Sit in a comfortable position. Relax. Let your eyes close and breathe in and out slowly three times. Invite your life into your awareness. Notice whatever experiences, feelings, or thoughts of interbeing come to mind. Stay with this for a while. When you feel ready, open your eyes.

PART FIVE

BODHICITTA

There is a baby Buddha in our store consciousness, and we have to give him or her a chance to be born. When we touch our baby Buddha—the seeds of understanding and love that are buried within us—we become filled with bodhicitta, the mind of enlightenment, the mind of love. From that moment on, everything we do or say nourishes the baby Buddha within us, and we are filled with joy, confidence, and energy. According to Mahayana Buddhism, awakening our bodhicitta, touching our mind of enlightenment, our mind of love, is the moment the practice begins.

—Thich Nhat Hanh,
Cultivating the Mind of Love

In keeping with his identification of enlightenment with mindfulness, Thầy sometimes referred to our baby Buddha as a "part-time Buddha." "When you drink your tea mindfully," he would say, "you're enlightened about drinking tea." Like many others, I live mindfully some of the time. When I do, I grow my bodhicitta, my mind of love and enlightenment.

Mindfulness, like all other seeds, manifests in mind consciousness when the causes and conditions are sufficient. It remains hidden in store consciousness when they aren't sufficient. Seeds of suffering, especially the seed of fear, may be so large that when they manifest in awareness, there's no room available for mindfulness.

In his Dharma talks, Thầy transmitted enormous bodhicitta through his stories, his humor, his smiles and laughter, his dancing energy—his very being! Having time with him and with others in touch with their inner Buddhas watered the bodhicitta of participants. However, not all were conscious of this, as the unhappiness of the woman in my 1992 Dharma discussion group made evident. Her expectations for a different kind of retreat seemed to prevent her from opening to receive Thầy's teaching, at least at the level of awareness. Because of their capacity to limit curiosity and close the heart, expectations, judgments, and thought are three of the greatest hindrances to receiving bodhicitta from others.

In this regard, Thầy taught the interbeing nature of transmitter, transmission, and receiver. This explains why each person received a different transmission during Thầy's Dharma talks. It also helps explain why his talks became stronger as retreats progressed and participants, rested up from busy lives and embraced by the collective bodhicitta of the Sangha, relaxed defenses and opened to the depth of Thầy's teaching—whether or not they fully understood it at the intellectual level.

With the exception of the monastics, few of us live immersed in bodhicitta in one of the communities Thầy founded. How can we care for our own seeds of awakening? When awakening becomes our volition, we naturally gravitate to other people on the path, to attending Sanghas, and going on retreats. Through practice we grow our capacity to look and listen deeply to ourselves and others—our suffering and our joy—and to observe, reflect upon, and contemplate life. As we become aware of the obstacles that impede bodhicitta's growth, we let go of them as best we can and, with practice, begin to release our fear and sense of separateness in space and time. And we nurture the baby Buddha in us by inviting our Buddha qualities, exemplified in the bodhisattvas described below. Plum Village ceremonies regularly include the practice of Invoking the Bodhisattvas'

Names [Appendix 4]. In this ceremony participants do prostrations as a succession of bodhisattvas are called upon. Avalokiteshvara, the bodhisattva of great compassion, is petitioned as follows in this invocation:

> *We invoke your name, Avalokiteshvara. We aspire to learn your way of listening in order to help relieve the suffering in the world. You know how to listen in order to understand. We invoke your name in order to practice listening with all our attention and openheartedness. We will sit and listen without any prejudice. We will sit and listen without judging or reacting. We will sit and listen in order to understand. We will sit and listen so attentively that we will be able to hear what the other person is saying and also what is being left unsaid. We know that just by listening deeply we already alleviate a great deal of pain and suffering in the other person.*[31]

Manjushri, the bodhisattva of great wisdom, Samantabhadra, the bodhisattva of great understanding, Kshitigarbha, the bodhisattva who works to save all beings, and Sadaparibhuta, the never-disparaging bodhisattva, are called upon in a similar manner. This practice waters and strengthens the seeds of these bodhisattva qualities and the bodhicitta present in our store consciousness.

Chapter 10

COMING ALIVE

Mindfulness must be engaged. Once there is seeing, there must be acting. Otherwise, what's the use of seeing?

–Thich Nhat Hanh,
Peace Is Every Step

Engaged Practice

During the 1990s I sign petitions and attend demonstrations with other Sangha members, but I don't feel drawn to become more deeply involved with social issues. My roles as teacher, spouse, father, and son consume most of my time. What's left I devote to the Sangha, to my practice, and to retreats that help support my balance. Nevertheless, as I regard other deeply engaged Sangha members, I feel as though I'm not doing enough. The fact that practicing in my family is engaged practice doesn't occur to me. After receiving lamp transmission and beginning to investigate how I might share Thầy's teachings with students and educators, I realize that both family life and teaching, when they nourish and are nourished by my bodhicitta, are engaged practice.

My seeds of awakening are being watered through my work as an educator. I've loved teaching from the beginning. Much more than a job, teaching becomes a vocation. I find my experience of teaching reflected in these words of mystic and theologian Howard Thurman:

> *Don't ask what the world needs. Ask what makes you come alive*
> *and go out and do it. Because what the world needs is people who*
> *have come alive.*[32]

Teaching makes me come alive. With no educators in my family, the causes and conditions fueling this passion take thirty years of teaching before I become aware of them. In January 2001, about halfway through a six-week personal retreat in Plum Village, I receive a call from Elisabeth. My brother is in the hospital with a grave medical condition and may be dying. Twenty-six years earlier, Quaker worship had supported my connection with Bob when he was hospitalized. This time I take refuge in the meditation hall after dinner, sitting alone in the vast silence. After many tears, the Buddha's teachings on interbeing and impermanence come to me. Bob's physical form, which manifested in 1947, might soon cease to be. At the same time, I understand that his nature isn't confined to this form. He will continue to live on in me and in others he has touched. I will be a part of Bob's "continuation." Then I see I'm already his continuation, that he's always been part of me. In fact, he was the inspiration behind my passion for helping young people. I return home with a deeper understanding of my vocation.

At the end of that year, 2001, Thầy honors teaching as my Dharmic work in the Plum Village lamp transmission ceremony. I will no longer be teaching only mathematics; I'll be sharing, as best I can, empowerment, relationship, and love. I'll be nourishing bodhicitta in my students.

Mindfulness at School

Although for many years I've begun my math classes at Sidwell with a moment of silence, I haven't regarded it as a spiritual practice. It was a way—in keeping with the silence of Meeting for Worship—of helping students fully arrive. And when I began reading Thầy's books to my math students in 1987, I intended nothing more than to share some practical wisdom from a wise elder. Even in 1989 when I received the Five Precepts from Thây and began to practice mindfulness with the Washington Mindfulness Community, it still didn't occur to me to share my practice with my students. After all, I was a math teacher at Sidwell. Mindfulness practice was a part of my personal life.

Then in the early 1990s, conditions prompt me to introduce yoga in one of my algebra classes. The students are having a hard time settling down to work. When I ask why, they tell me that our class meets right after lunch and they're tired. That makes sense. I thank them for their candor and promise to look for a solution over the upcoming holiday break.

I spend part of the break at the Bhavana Society's retreat center in West Virginia, a hundred miles west of DC, where one of the monks, Bhante Rahula, teaches yoga. Responding to my question, he shares a practice that he suggests will bring *chi*—life force energy—up from the feet.

"Stand on your toes with your hands over your head," he instructs. "Breathe out as you bend down and touch the floor. Then breathe in and slowly raise your hands back up over your head. Repeat this nine more times, remaining on your toes."

When I return to my after-lunch algebra class, I gather the students in a circle and lead them in the exercise. They are immediately invigorated. "In the future," I say, "we'll start each class this way. I'll ask you to take turns leading it. If you're fully awake and ready for class, participation in the exercise will be optional." For the rest of the year almost everyone joins the circle. Passersby peer in with questioning looks. The novelty becomes the signature of our class, and we become something of a practice community. Best of all, students are more focused on work and more attentive to me and each other. Introducing this yogic practice was totally organic. Normally, I don't consider bringing mindfulness practice to school.

Several years later, fate intervenes again. As the school year begins, I attend a meeting for new teachers where I caution them about taking on too many volunteer jobs. Afterward Ann, an experienced teacher, tells me that even without extra duties, life at school is far too full. I agree, then suggest, "Every time we see each other this year, no matter where we are, what we're doing, or where we're going, let's stop, smile to each other and breathe in and out slowly three times." Ann isn't a meditator, nor is she familiar with mindfulness, but the idea appeals to her. We honor our agreement all year and grow closer in the process. Eventually Ann asks how this idea occurred to me. I tell her about mindfulness and how we use a bell as an invitation to stop and return to the present moment: "We've been human bells of mindfulness for each other. Smiling is also an important part of my tradition." This strikes a chord in Ann. She wants to know more. She begins attending days of mindfulness and mindfulness retreats on her own, then with members of her family, developing her own practice.

Vigor

Ann sets something in motion that crystallizes in the winter of 1999–2000. I'm reading *The Seven Stages of Money Maturity* by George Kinder. The stage that he calls *vigor* gets my attention. He explains that work contains vigor if it returns as much or more energy as you put into it. He then invites us to meditate on work that has this quality. Two instances come to my mind—teaching problem-solving at a gifted and talented summer program and conducting a conflict-resolution seminar at Sidwell. Does my math teaching have vigor? I enjoy it, do a good job, and have no sign of burnout, but at the end of each year I'm tired. Summer vacations recharge me. I could continue in this way until I retire, but do I want to perpetuate this pattern? Or do I want to go for vigor? I make an appointment to talk with School Head Bruce Stewart and explain that I'd like to refresh my spiritual life through a yearlong leave of absence. Bruce asks if I plan to return the next year. I say, "Yes."

At that moment I do plan to return, but I honestly have no idea whether a year away from teaching will change my mind.

As spring wears on and I still have no plans for my time away, I begin to feel uneasy. What if the year passes and I don't discover my passion? Then I get the idea to go to Parker Palmer's new Center for Teacher Formation to train to be a facilitator. When I tell Elisabeth, she says, "That's Parker's work, Richard. You need to find your own work." I know she's right. I continue living with the uncertainty. Later in the spring my friend Sue-Anne calls from upstate New York, lamenting the tremendous pressures experienced by both students and teachers. "Someone ought to teach them meditation," I tell her. As I hear the words come out of my mouth, I know that someone is me. I've hit on my new direction, offering mindfulness retreats for teachers.

The sum of my prior experience is co-leading two Quaker retreats with Elisabeth in the 1990s. Elisabeth is an experienced retreat leader, undergirded by a strong Quaker foundation. At her retreats, I share mindfulness exercises and lead guided meditations. By spring 2000, I've practiced mindfulness for eleven years, but I feel far from confident about teaching it. The mindfulness practices with my algebra students and Ann arose naturally. Now I need to come up with a curriculum. Where do I begin? I have no idea how to organize this kind of program. I'll need a co-leader.

David Mallery, an encouraging mentor and friend, routinely organizes workshops. I'll tell him what I want to do and hope he'll invite me to lead one of his programs. When I call, he's enthusiastic. "Where would you like to lead a retreat?" he asks.

I hadn't thought about this, but without hesitation I say, "Pendle Hill."

That would be perfect for what you have in mind," he responds.

"But I'd like to co-lead it with someone," I continue.

"Sorry, I can't help you with that," David says.

I call Shirley Dodson, the person in charge of scheduling Pendle Hill weekend programs. After hearing my proposal, Shirley tells me that this is the type of event Pendle Hill would like to offer. "We still have an unscheduled weekend in October. I'll be sending out the brochure with next fall's programs soon. Can you get me a description of the retreat with your bio and a head shot by Friday?"

This is happening way too fast. It's May. October is just around the corner.

"But I'd like a co-leader, and I don't know who that will be."

"No problem," she says. "We can add a second leader later."

At home that night I consider the mindfulness practitioners I know. Susan Murphy comes to mind. She would be ideal. Susan is a Quaker, also a member of Thich Nhat Hanh's Order of Interbeing, and a professor at San Jose State University. I leave a message on her phone. When I arrive at school the next day, there's an email from Susan, enthusiastically accepting my invitation.

Mindfulness with Teachers

Although Susan and I have both practiced mindfulness for some years, neither of us has taught it. There is no mindfulness curriculum or guidelines that we know of. We decide to offer a menu of practices and exercises for reflection and sharing. Since our Pendle Hill students will range from kindergarten teachers to university professors with varied mindfulness backgrounds, we'll use an inclusive approach.

It comes as no surprise when we teach it that participants most appreciate the eating and walking meditations. These can happen anywhere during their day. Since we practice these meditations together, each participant is supported by the others—the power of Sangha. They also enjoy sitting individually outdoors for twenty minutes with eyes closed, just listening. When we gather indoors, one teacher excitedly reports hearing a leaf fall for the first time.

Susan and I lead two more retreats before we both realize that cross-country travel coupled with full teaching loads isn't sustainable. Fortunately, I've recently met Irene McHenry, the new executive director of the Friends Council on Education, at Susan's and my second Pendle Hill retreat. With years of mindfulness experience, Irene offers her support. For the next five years, with the blessing of strong teamwork, Irene and I co-lead mindfulness retreats for educators at Pendle Hill. I've received no mindfulness teacher training for this work with Susan and Irene or for the teaching I give students. However, after eleven years of practicing with Thich Nhat Hanh in Plum Village, attending his American retreats, and practicing weekly with the Washington Mindfulness Community, I feel it in my bones.

Mindfulness with Students

I'm blessed with support for my new venture with mindfulness in education from a new mentor, Paula Lawrence-Wehmiller. I was profoundly moved by a presentation she gave at a David Mallery workshop in Philadelphia some years before. More recently I heard her speak at the Washington National Cathedral. In the interim she'd ordained as an Episcopal priest. I was excited to hear that she offered spiritual direction for teachers.

Now, a few years later, as I begin sharing mindfulness in schools, I feel in need of counsel. I can create programs alright, but I need some assistance in seeing the big picture and how I fit into it. I contact Paula for spiritual direction, and we set up monthly phone calls. Paula listens for half an hour, then asks questions, shares a relevant poem or tells me a story from her life that illuminates just where in this new adventure I find myself.

During my year of exploration, I'm invited by several schools to teach mindfulness. Following an after-school workshop for interested faculty members at Friends School Mullica Hill in New Jersey, several teachers invite me to visit their classes. The teacher retreats boost my confidence. Now I'm optimistic that I can come up with mindfulness lessons that work for students.

The teacher of a twelfth-grade religion class asks me to help prepare students for what they'll soon encounter studying events leading up to the Holocaust. I advise the class that mindfulness practice can help us be present with others' and our own suffering without becoming overwhelmed. Describing the process of holding emotions in our awareness with great tenderness, like a mother cradling a crying infant, I invite students to choose personal experiences of "small" suffering from their own lives—an argument with a friend or a disappointing test score. If the event is small, I explain, our mindfulness will be strong enough to hold it. After leading a guided meditation focused on the breath, I ask them to bring their small suffering into their awareness and to hold it gently for five minutes. The room falls silent. Afterward, several students share their experiences. Overall they are surprised at how useful this practice has been. One boy shares the discovery that his suffering is not as small as he'd thought.

I go on to a third-grade class where we mindfully eat chocolate chip cookies. All goes well, but I have no clue what approach to use with a ninth-grade English class. I start by introducing myself, letting the students know I teach high school math as well as meditation to students and teachers. Then I ask, "Why would your teacher invite me to teach you meditation?" A number of hands shoot up. I take notes as students respond and let them guide me in shaping my remarks and choice of visualizations.

One student suggests it might be because the class tends to be restless. I follow up on this great opening with the meditation I used when I began to practice:

Breathing in, I know I am breathing in.
Breathing out, I know I am breathing out.
Breathing in, my breath grows deep.
Breathing out, my breath grows slow.
Breathing in, I feel calm.

Breathing out, I feel ease in my body.
Breathing in, I smile.
Breathing out, I release.
Dwelling in the present moment,
I know it is a wonderful moment.[33]

It fits the moment perfectly.

Upon my return to Sidwell after this year-long sabbatical, I'm invited to teach a class on stress reduction as part of the health unit in Freshman Studies. Sidwell, like so many schools, can be stressful. Here families have high expectations for their children and for the school. The environment at New Trier, my own high school in Illinois, was similar. I think about my brother's emotional and physical disorders and wonder if they are stress related. I think of him as I plan my class.

Stress

Freshman Studies is required of all ninth graders at Sidwell. I plan to base the stress-reduction class I'll offer on mindfulness. It won't be easy to get students engaged. I recall Frank McCourt's advice in *Teacher Man*, describing unmotivated high school English students. "What is it they're interested in?" he asks himself; and the answers are immediate: sex and food. He introduces a hugely successful unit in which students collect and recite family recipes, some with musical accompaniment. I know I need students to "buy in," but asking young people to fully attend to something with curiosity and non-judgmental awareness is asking them to care and be vulnerable, no small "ask" in the face of possible scoffing and ridicule.

I consider McCourt's question: "What interests them?" At their age, young people are figuring out who they are. They're interested primarily in themselves, their peers, and their bodies. For them, the mind is a new frontier. I decide to invite them to watch what their minds do when they're at rest. Riffing on Shakespeare, I call it "mind as a stage."

I begin by suggesting that our minds play a significant role in our well-being: "When I talk about mind, I'm talking about awareness. Think of your awareness as a 'stage.' On your stage, a series of actors—thoughts, feelings, perceptions, and sensations—will make appearances."

Once the students are physically and emotionally comfortable in their seats, I ask them to close their eyes or leave them slightly open and tune into whatever appears on their stage. "Just watch. Whatever thoughts, feelings, perceptions, or sensations arise during the next few minutes, simply *observe*. Don't let yourself get carried away by anything you see."

After five minutes, the students slowly open their eyes. The room feels permeated by silence. Slowly, I ask a series of questions: How many of you were aware of physical sensations—sounds, smells, tastes, contact with your seats, heartbeat, breathing, feet, or other body parts? How many of you were aware of emotions? Thoughts? How many of you saw a thought arise? A thought end? How many of you experienced negative thoughts or feelings? Of these, how many had to do with events that have already happened, incidents you felt upset or guilty about? Many hands go up. How many negative thoughts and feelings had to do with the future, things they're anxious about? This also gets a big response. Finally, I ask, "How many of your negative thoughts and feelings have to do with the present?" Two hands are raised.

I point out that what you just witnessed your minds doing during this five-minute "performance" is repeated about 70,000 times in the course of a year. You can understand why the mind plays such a significant role in creating how you feel, including stress and tension. If you're aware of the negative thoughts and feelings that fill your mind and if you can develop ways to replace them with positive thoughts and feelings, you can live a happier, less anxious life in and out of school.

I give the students an image—the mind as a cable TV with many channels—the anger channel, the peace channel, the love channel, the anxiety channel, and so on. We all have these channels. What differs from one person to the next is the signal strength of particular channels. Each of us has one or two strong, default channels, ones that our minds tune to regularly, regardless of what may be happening in the moment.

Even if the signal strength of your anxiety channel is weak, it may show up when your math teacher announces a pop quiz. Meditation is a way to help your mind turn to positive channels.

Stress Reduction

Next I share about reading *The Miracle of Mindfulness,* and subsequently hearing about meditation from a high school senior, Chris. I tell the ninth graders I'd recounted this story at an assembly at Sidwell, concluding the assembly with a two-minute sitting meditation. A few days later, Audrey, a twelfth grader, offered this message at our all-school Meeting for Worship:

"I've been thinking about the fact that the main change Mr. Brady's student noticed in himself after he'd been meditating on a regular basis was that he was less angry. Lately I've been so angry myself because I've had all this resentment building up inside over responsibilities that I have to fulfill. I really want to let it all go, but I can't. This makes me even more resentful and angry. The other night I was sitting at my desk around 12:30 a.m., completely stressing because I had so much work to do. I was on the verge of breaking. But I just closed my eyes and took in ten deep breaths, concentrating on my inhaling and exhaling the whole time. When I opened my eyes, I was so relaxed. If any of you are stressed out or angry, just take ten seconds to close your eyes and breathe. The action is so little, but the reward is tremendous."[34]

Audrey's story provides a good opening for me to invite this group of freshmen to practice meditation. I lead them in a ten-minute guided visualization:

Breathing in, I know I am breathing in.
Breathing out, I know I am breathing out.

Breathing in, I see myself as a flower.
Breathing out, I feel fresh.

Breathing in, I see myself as a mountain.
Breathing out, I feel solid.

Breathing in, I see myself as still water.
Breathing out, I reflect things as they truly are.

Breathing in, I see myself as space.
Breathing out, I feel free.[35]

This short introduction underlines the importance of tuning in to positive channels to replace negative ones. Daily meditation can strengthen the signal of positive channels which might eventually become their default channels. From 2001 through 2009, I introduce mindfulness in this way to all of Sidwell's ninth graders.

MiEN

I'm introverted by nature, so it's a giant leap for me to venture forth from Sidwell Friends to lead retreats and teach mindfulness in other schools. But I'm motivated during several of Thầy's retreats to organize meetings for educators in which we introduce ourselves with a few words about our work with mindfulness. In 2001, with a special appeal to educators, Thầy offers two five-day retreats—one in Massachusetts and one in California. At the start of one of his Dharma talks at the University of Massachusetts, Thầy invites the educators present to sit near him during one of the Dharma talks. He begins by advising the fifty of us to turn our classes into Sanghas. Inspired, I reserve a large classroom at UMass for two teacher get-togethers during the retreat. Many of us feel immense gratitude when we discover other pioneers on this frontier.

Mindfulness is not yet a buzzword. It is not yet featured on the covers of national magazines. Mindfulness training for teachers doesn't exist. Most of us know no other educators who share our mutual interest. Suddenly we've come together in community! We want to stay in touch. I collect names and email addresses, then contact two West Coast friends to suggest they do the same at Thầy's retreat in California. On October 18, 2001, the Mindfulness in Education Network (MiEN) is born as an email listserv with seventy-eight participants.[36] Soon MiEN launches a website for sharing our new movement worldwide. MiEN's listserv whets my appetite for an in-person community of mindful educators. This is just a taste. I want a whole meal.

In 2006, Amy Saltzman, founder of MiEN's sister organization, the Association for Mindfulness in Education (AME), invites Rob Wall (a fellow student of Thầy's), Irene McHenry, and me to present at AME's first conference in San Francisco. The day before the gathering, we join the other presenters for practice and conversation. We're all invigorated. Amy suggests that MiEN offer a similar conference on the East Coast. Who among us has the time to coordinate that? I do, but only after I retire in 2007.

Then, with the support of Irene, Rob, and Amy, I organize a one-day conference at Sidwell Friends in February 2008. It's attended by 160 people that year and turns into an annual gathering. Subsequently held on a variety of college campuses, MiEN's conference expands to three days with a daylong opening workshop, an evening keynote talk, a symposium, and a closing day of mindfulness practice for conferees. MiEN invites people with various mindfulness backgrounds who work in diverse areas of education all over the world to join our listserv and attend our conference. By 2017, MiEN's listserv has grown to more than 1,700. Thousands more visit the MiEN website to join our listserv, watch videos of plenary speakers from past conferences, and examine resources.

Chapter 11

DHARMA TEACHER

The problem that faces us is the problem of awakening. What we lack is not an ideology or doctrine that will save the world. What we lack is mindfulness of what we are, of what our situation really is. We need to wake up in order to rediscover our human sovereignty. We are riding a horse that is running out of control. The way of salvation is a new culture in which human beings are encouraged to rediscover their deepest nature.

—Thich Nhat Hanh,
Zen Keys: A Guide to Zen

Lamp Transmission

When I become a Dharma teacher in 2001, Thầy not only presents me with a lamp whose flame is lit from the flame of his own lamp, he also presents me with a poem he has written for me, as is the tradition with a new Dharma teacher:

A Dharma rain penetrates the realm of the heart.
A great Bridge helps reestablish deep love.
Tending the precious flowers every day
helps purify all layers of society.

Dharma Bridge, the name Thầy gave me in 1992, appears in the first lines of the poem. I received this name as confirmation of my calling to share the Dharma in non-Buddhist settings. After reciting the poem, Thầy explains that the "precious flowers" are my students. Moved by his understanding, I weep. But what am I to teach? Mindfulness practice is more than relieving stress. It must lead to insight.

Insight

According to the Buddha's teachings, insight arises in two stages: *samatha*, stopping and calming, and *vipassana*, looking deeply. I think about my own experiences. As I was getting to know Thầy in the early 1990s, I participated in a week-long meditation program at Kripalu Yoga Center in Lenox, Massachusetts. The instructor there had attended a rigorous ten-day Buddhist meditation retreat in the tradition of Indian teacher S. N. Goenka. Basing his instruction on that experience, he asks us to follow our breath in and out of our nostrils for forty-five minutes at a time. His strict instruction earns him the nickname "Sarge." Toward the end of the program, just before a meditation class, I enjoy a vigorous shiatsu bodywork session with one of the center's healing arts practitioners. Then, settling into a seated posture, I focus on inhaling and exhaling. For the next forty-five minutes I stay focused on my nostrils. Not a single thought crosses my mind. Afterward I realize I've reached a pinnacle in my practice. I'm soon disillusioned. I've had tranquil experiences since then, but none close to that forty-five minutes of uninterrupted focus.

Some people are drawn to Buddhist practice primarily for calming. I love sitting in silent Buddhist and Quaker settings to calm my mind. But this is only the first stage of meditation, a prerequisite to the second stage, vipassana, or looking deeply. This is not an intellectual process or philosophical reflection. It involves simply holding whatever is present—an emotion or a particular thought or image—in mindful awareness. From this holding, an insight along with a shift in perspective may arise. Quakers speak of "waiting worship," quelling ordinary thinking and waiting to receive the still, small voice of Spirit or the inward teacher. I find the two practices to be close. I sometimes experience deep, preverbal insights during Buddhist meditation and Quaker worship, not the result of thinking or reflecting. Those insights are intellectual, mediated by thought and language. Deeper insights are nonverbal and often accompany a shift in my perspective toward some facet of life—a friendship, an illness, or an emotional state such as loneliness. I may be able to say something about it, but the words come afterward.

Fostering Insight

I'm hoping to share insight practices with students and teachers, but no opportunities arise. I stay attentive to MiEN's listserv. Through a post from the Center for Contemplative Mind in Society, I discover a network of academics using contemplative methods in their teaching. In February 2005, I attend a conference aimed at teaching contemplative practices, sponsored by the Center for the Professional Education of Teachers at Teachers College, Columbia University. Nearly two hundred people from all levels of education attend. The educators describe courses, such as one in Buddhist psychology, where students study contemplative practices. In others, such as improvisational jazz, students develop more presence in playing their music. In a creative writing course, students are invited to employ mindfulness in the process of writing poems.

In the closing talk entitled "Love and Knowledge," physics professor Arthur Zajonc of Amherst College describes a course he and art historian Joel Upton offer together. They teach various forms of contemplation to help students develop insight. The students, he tells us, react to the course with gratitude. This is what I've been looking for. I leave hopeful about the future of education.

During the conference, Mirabai Bush, director of the Center, announces a week-long summer workshop at Smith College on contemplative curriculum development. Inspired by Arthur Zajonc's talk, I feel drawn to attend—eager to develop contemplative methods for Math II, the honors geometry course at Sidwell Friends. If we contemplate geometric figures in a mindful way, will we uncover new insights? I hope so, although I'm unsure what methods I might employ.

Both my department head and principal have faith in my ability to develop something of merit. They support my application for the workshop and my intention to add a contemplative dimension to the course. I thank them and, at the same time, warn them that students and parents may feel that this new component of Math II doesn't provide adequate preparation for subsequent coursework. I spend the summer anticipating the workshop with both excitement and anxiety. I don't know what the new Math II will look like.

In preparation I attend a retreat with Thây near Boston. Besides helping me slow down and settle more deeply into a contemplative frame of mind, this retreat gives me a chance to participate in a special interest group with other educators. In one of our meetings, several teachers say they dread the coming school year. Referring to the No Child Left Behind Act and state-mandated testing, they question the possibility of ever teaching the "whole child." Another group member responds with a verse from Woody Guthrie's "This Land Is Your Land": "As I was walking, I saw a sign there. And that sign said. No Trespassing. But on the other side it didn't say nothing. That side was made for you and me!"[37] He goes on to suggest we look at the other side of No Child Left Behind. Its intent—for all children to learn—is a goal we all support. If we teach with integrity, addressing the whole child, our students will meet mandated standards and much more. As I listen to him, I begin to envision the contemplative geometry course I will teach in the fall. I'm feeling excited to begin.

Following the retreat with Thầy, my entry into the contemplative curriculum development workshop at Smith is seamless. During the opening circle, we share aspirations for incorporating meditative approaches in our courses. Two professors relate that, with some fear of consequences, they'd employed contemplative methods the previous year. In both cases they were surprised to receive the highest marks of their career on student evaluations. During the days that follow, we explore mindfulness techniques we might use in our courses. We practice yoga, sitting meditation, and movement daily. We hear stimulating talks from leaders in the field and share questions, ideas, and resources.

True to our deepest selves, and regardless of how contemplative pedagogy is seen by our colleagues back home, we generate a mountain of energy and enthusiasm. During an evening of poems, stories, and music, I read Martha Graham's advice to her sister dancer, Agnes de Mille: "There is a vitality, a life force, an energy, a quickening, that is translated through you into action, and because there is only one of you in all time, this expression is unique. And if you block it, it will never exist through any other medium and will be lost."[38] These words speak passionately to my own aspirations. May it be so.

I return home with a few new ideas about teaching mindfulness and a deep sense of trust in the process. Still, I know I have a lot to learn and will certainly make mistakes. Only time will tell if my students reap the benefits. But I'm clear about the value of these methods and certain that my confidence will shine throughout the school year. I will grow, alongside my students, as a learner.

Math II

I commence Math II with an exercise in mindful eating. Based on a well-known exercise introduced by Jon Kabat-Zinn, I give each student three raisins and ask them to take a full five minutes to eat them mindfully. Each subsequent class begins with a five-minute contemplative activity. Before tests and quizzes, I lead a two-part guided meditation. Part I helps students get in touch with their feelings. Part II helps them focus on a positive math experience. On days when students arrive tired, we begin with yoga stretching to refresh our energy.

On the first day of class, I hand out journals and ask students to keep them in the classroom until the end of the year, not to take them home. Sometimes I invite them to work on a challenging problem in their journals or write about some aspect of the course. I read them at the end of the week and write, "Thank you. RB." My appreciation is the most important message I can give. Most Fridays we practice free writing. The students and I write continuously in our journals for five minutes, putting on paper whatever is on our minds. Other days we respond to prompts such as short stories from wisdom traditions, poems, or quotations. Students do that writing in the back of their journals with the understanding that I will not read it. I soon recognize that journal writing is the practice I like most.

Hanoi

Including mindfulness practices in math class makes my final two years of teaching the most satisfying of my career. I enjoy new vitality fueled by the practice. Still, I realize that I'm ready to stop. I want to share mindfulness with the world of education. After my 2007 retirement, Thầy announces he's been invited by the Vietnamese government to be the keynote speaker at the 2008 United Nations Day of Vesak celebration in Hanoi. The theme will be "Buddhist Contributions to Building a Just, Democratic and Civilized Society." Education is one of seven areas to be addressed. Thầy accepts the invitation on the condition that he be allowed to offer a week-long retreat in Hanoi prior to the celebration. After decades in exile, Thầy first returned to Vietnam in 2005. This will be his third trip with students from around the world. I want to be one of them.

I think about possible topics for a paper I might present in Hanoi. Most attending the celebration will be monastic and lay Buddhists. A paper based on Buddhist teachings would be appropriate for this setting. Presenting a paper will be a new and stimulating challenge for me. I settle on the topic of the Buddha's teachings on the seven factors of enlightenment (diligence, concentration, joy, relaxation, curiosity, equanimity, and mindfulness). I've explicitly nurtured these factors in my students during my last two years of teaching. With the exception of curiosity, I've felt successful.

American education seems headed in the opposite direction, and I suspect Southeast Asian education is no different. My proposal is accepted. I begin the paper, entitled "Realizing True Education with Mindfulness,"[39] by describing the challenges to each of the seven factors faced by educators. Then I share how I used mindfulness in my teaching to support the other six enlightenment factors. I include students' statements about each factor, two poems, and a guided meditation that encourages contemplation. I'm invited to present my paper at *Vesak*, the Southeast Asia celebration commemorating the Buddha's birth, enlightenment, and death all rolled into one.

Before Thầy gives his keynote address on the first day, he invites the 400 laypeople who are on retreat with him to join 100 monastics from his affiliated Bat Nha Monastery in the central highlands of Vietnam to stand behind him on the stage. With all of us standing there, he silently pours himself a cup of tea and drinks it slowly. Then, he invites the large temple bell to sound and leads us in chanting *Namo Avalokiteshvara*, invoking the name of the bodhisattva of compassion.[40] This moving chant encourages chanters and listeners to allow the energy of compassion to arise within them. The chanting continues for twenty minutes. Written by a Plum Village practitioner, this chant is familiar to us but unfamiliar to the several thousand Asian monastics in attendance. As tears stream down my face, I notice a yellow-robed monk near the front of the audience looking bored, probably waiting for Thầy to begin his keynote address. I focus my compassion in his direction.

The following day, I deliver my paper. I begin with four minutes of free writing, a shock to this primarily Vietnamese audience. Later I invite their contemplation of a poem, followed by sharing in pairs, another format they find unfamiliar. I receive only two questions during the Q&A that follows. An Asian monk asks me about the role of chanting in the Plum Village tradition. It's a practice to open the heart, I respond. Another monastic asks about the relationship between the Plum Village and Theravadin traditions. Though different in form, they lead to the same truths, I reply. Most of the audience members seem primarily interested in monastic education. I look forward to opportunities to share my paper with lay educators.

Dharma Teachers

While I'm writing about the Dharma's role in education and occasionally sharing it directly with educators, a group of my Dharma teacher friends have organized the North American Dharma Teachers Sangha (NADTS). Among their committees are groups to help standardize mentoring procedures for Order of Interbeing aspirants, to identify worthy candidates for lamp transmission, and to make resources available to practitioners and Sanghas who seek support. I feel awkward not being more involved in the NADTS, but I'm comforted by Thây's blessing of my work in education. Finally in 2014, I travel to Deer Park Monastery in Escondido, California, to attend NADTS's third biennial gathering. I'd missed the first two because the MiEN conferences occurred at the same time. Before long I'm handed a sheet with a list of committees and asked how I'd like to contribute. None of the topics speak to me. I hold on to the sheet.

During a free moment, a friend approaches, concerned about Dharma talks that contain only impersonal explications of the Buddha's teachings. I ask her to say more. She wants to help Dharma teachers find their own voices, she says. We all grew up listening to Thây's inspirational talks. None of us can do what he does. My

Dharma talks are quite different, I tell her. They often involve exercises—guided meditations, journaling, or sharing in pairs or a group rather than didactic teaching. I think of my friends, Letizia and Stefano, the two Dharma teachers who hosted my retreat in Italy the previous summer. At that time Letizia and Stefano had not yet begun to teach. Recently, they told me they'll be leading their first retreat. They both had difficulty when they thought of giving a Dharma talk until they discovered my more experiential approach.

Of the twenty-five lay Dharma teachers gathered at Deer Park, I know two others who have careers in education. The three of us have benefited from our classroom experience, but we all have much to learn about teaching the Dharma. Suddenly I'm clear about what I want to contribute to my fellow teachers. On the committee preference form, I write: "I want to serve on a committee that nourishes the teaching of Dharma teachers." Later in the year I'm invited to join the newly formed Dharma Teachers Life and Nourishment Committee. We meet by conference call monthly to look at a broad range of ways to support and encourage Dharma teachers.

At the next gathering of the NADTS, our committee divides participants into two groups based on length of experience as a Dharma teacher. Then we propose a reflection and ask two questions:

> Consider benefits you have received from Dharma teachers from the Plum Village lineage and from other significant teachers. Please reflect silently on the most skillful means they demonstrated.

> With appreciation that we all are increasingly skilled in sharing the Dharma, what are your growing edges and/or aspirations pertaining to the Dharma teaching in which you currently engage or in which you hope to engage in the future?

> Based on the growing edges and aspirations expressed in your groups, how might the Dharma teacher Sangha support the further flourishing of our fellow teachers?

As the facilitator, I watch these exceptional teachers quietly contemplate *their* special teachers. The silence is profound. As we turn our attention to sharing our own pedagogy, aspirations flow slowly and softly among us. The intimacy of connection deepens. Our Dharma teacher family is ripening. A minority of our seventy Dharma teachers are present, but I hope with support from our committee, we'll all continue to grow.

A Dharma Talk

When I was ordained as a Dharma teacher, it became my privilege and challenge to pass on Thây's teachings. All his teachings are meant to be *practiced*. Although I've focused on offering my teaching to students and educators, I occasionally offer days of mindfulness and co-lead regional New England retreats after moving to Vermont. When I return to DC to visit, I sometimes offer Dharma talks to the Washington Mindfulness Community. The following story recounts one way I try to share a lived understanding of Thây's teaching about Sangha with my root Sangha five years after Elisabeth and I move to Vermont.

> It is probable that the next Buddha will not take the form
> of an individual. The next Buddha may take the form of
> a community, a community practicing understanding and
> loving kindness, a community practicing mindful living.[41]
>
> —Thich Nhat Hanh

This quote is with me as I prepare to return to Washington, DC. I've been honored with a request from the WMC to offer a Dharma talk. I know I'm missed, but my years of teaching assure me the community doesn't need a sage on the stage. I suggest that, instead of a talk, I conduct a question-and-answer session. Rather than a traditional

Q&A, I'd like it to be one that will tap the wisdom of the whole community.

As a young math teacher, I had similar concerns. Eventually I gave up lecturing and began asking students to work together in small groups. Students shared their understanding of the math with several others, sometimes with the whole class, but the questions they worked on were ones I posed, not their own. When I did invite students to develop their own questions about the material, they almost always focused on facts. I'd never found a way to encourage them to ask deeper questions.

In mindfulness settings, when I've conducted Q&A sessions in the past, I've asked that questions be ones whose answers could benefit both the questioner's and others' practice. The small number of questions asked verbally or submitted in writing beforehand often dealt with personal issues that might benefit some others. This time in DC I ask *everyone* to write two questions about practice, one on each side of a three-by-five card, and deposit the card in the large, bowl-shaped bell in the front of the room. Twenty-four people submit cards. Then each person reaches into the bell, selects a card at random, reads its two questions, and circles the one that has the greatest appeal. Next, pairs of people share their selected questions with one another and together select the question they think best. After that each pair shares their selected question with another pair, and each group of four agrees on a single question which they then give to me. After just a few minutes, forty-eight questions are winnowed down to six.

After I read the selections aloud, each group of four discusses a different question, and someone from the group shares the group's collective answer. Questions include how to practice with a broken heart and how to practice with inner criticism. Everyone appreciates the spirited interactive process and the sharing of community wisdom.

Chapter 12

HEART WORK

A teacher cannot give you the truth. The truth is already in you. You only need to open yourself—body, mind and heart—so that his or her teachings will penetrate your own seeds of understanding and enlightenment. If you let the words enter you, the soil and the seeds will do the rest of the work.

–Thich Nhat Hanh,
The Heart of the Buddha's Teachings

European Institute of Applied Buddhism

In the spring of 2011, I receive a request from Sr. Annabel for a copy of *Tuning In: Mindfulness in Teaching and Learning,* a collection of stories by teachers about using mindfulness in the classroom that Irene McHenry and I curated for the Friends Council on Education. Thầy has proposed a three-level initiative called Applied Ethics for sharing Plum Village practice with teachers and students.[42] In August, Sr. Annabel and Sr. Jewel will co-teach Level I, a mindfulness course focused on helping teachers care for themselves and deepen their own practice, at Thich Nhat Hanh's European Institute of Applied Buddhism (EIAB) in Waldbröl, Germany.

I send Sr. Annabel the book and follow up with an offer of help. She accepts with pleasure. The course includes two meetings focused on sharing mindfulness practices with students. Other elements of the course, supported by the monastic community, are similar to Plum Village retreats. The mornings begin with meditation led by the monastics. These times include sutra reading, touching-the-earth meditations in which we connect physically through prostrations with teachings of the Buddha, and, toward the end of the course, a Five Mindfulness Trainings transmission ceremony similar to the ceremony at Omega Institute in 1989 where I received the precepts. We practice outdoor walking meditation together as a group and eat meals with the monastics in silence, exchanging smiles. From 9:00 p.m. until after breakfast, we observe Noble Silence—a time of no talking so we can connect with ourselves and others from a place of stillness.

Hearts are moved and lives are changed. Held by the mature practice of the monastic Sangha, our retreat group forms its own family to share sufferings, joys, wisdom, and playfulness. We find the teachings freeing. We hope the teachers will continue to develop and deepen their own practice before deciding what to share with others. In the future, this course will be offered at Thây's monasteries and during monastic retreat tours, but there is a conundrum. Small retreats are able to reach only a tiny percentage of all teachers worldwide, and the retreat setting can be a problem for those who are ill at ease with Buddhist ritual. At the same time, the monastic environment supports conditions for deep learning. I wonder how Thây's teachings might reach a larger number of teachers and students.

Level II is called "Teaching Mindfulness and Applied Ethics to Students." There is no model for a Level II training for teachers yet, nor is there a Plum Village curriculum. We will have to wait until the conditions are favorable for a model to manifest.

Upon returning home, I receive an email from my friend Meena Srinavasan, an Order of Interbeing member. Her proposal to present Thich Nhat Hanh's education program at a Garrison Institute symposium has been accepted. However, she's just discovered she has a scheduling conflict and needs someone to take her place. My MiEN comrade Rob Wall and I volunteer.

Designing the poster for the symposium, we highlight Thây's special role in teaching. Just as Thây has influenced countless Buddhist and non-Buddhist teachers, we see that applied ethics can flourish where teachers are already integrating mindfulness into education. The placard we design for the poster session reads, in large letters THICH NHAT HANH'S APPLIED ETHICS: WE ARE HERE FOR YOU. It goes on to display the Five Mindfulness Trainings, future educator events with Thây in Plum Village and London, and the schedule of the recent EIAB course with a photo of smiling participants and quotes from their evaluations:

I haven't felt this good about being a teacher in a long, long time.

—Teacher from Belgium

During the retreat, I gained the insight that no one can make me happy except myself.

—Teacher from Germany

My insight from this retreat: I thought about the specialness of food. When I would eat a piece of bell pepper, I would normally think, "Ah, a piece of pepper, I already know that taste and form." But now it occurs to me that in fact each bell pepper is new and different, and each bell pepper is only eaten once, however much it might resemble former and future peppers. The same of course is true for rain droplets or the smile of someone you know: each one is unique. I realize that we mechanically take things for granted, especially when we are not mindful.

—Teacher from Holland

Standing by the poster at the Garrison Institute, Rob and I chat with many interested folks. People report that they've read Thây's books for years. Some have been with him at public lectures or retreats. Thirty educators sign up to receive more information on applied ethics. Most show an interest in courses or retreats at one of the monasteries and are enthused about possible course offerings in the United States.

Centro Avalokita

After teaching at the EIAB and presenting at Garrison, I realize that what I have to offer teachers is best shared in Buddhist settings. I want to teach where I can bring my full spiritual self. In 2013, I'm invited to lead an eight-day educators' retreat at Centro Avalokita, a lay practice center in the tradition of Plum Village near Castelli, Italy. There I give eight Dharma talks, each simultaneously translated into Italian. Borrowing from my previous educator retreats, we all introduce ourselves by relating gifts we have to offer to the retreat.[43] We share many joyful moments, most memorably when we learn the words of Irving Berlin's "Blue Skies" and sing along with Frank Sinatra before contemplating blue-sky moments in our own lives.[44]

There are new challenges. I learn from facilitators that some of the retreatants do not understand a poem I read about leaving space when building campfires. I worry that people new to the practice might be even more confused by Thây's poem about interbeing "Please Call Me by My True Names,"[45] which I plan to offer later in the week.

PLEASE CALL ME BY MY TRUE NAMES

Don't say that I will depart tomorrow—
even today I am still arriving.
Look deeply: every second I am arriving
to be a bud on a spring branch,
to be a tiny bird, with still fragile wings,
learning to sing in my new nest,

to be a caterpillar in the heart of a flower,
to be a jewel hiding itself in a stone.

I still arrive, in order to laugh and to cry,
 to fear and to hope.
The rhythm of my heart is the birth and death
of all that is alive.

I am the mayfly metamorphosing
on the surface of the river.
And I am the bird
that swoops down to swallow the mayfly.

I am the frog swimming happily
in the clear water of a pond.
And I am the grass-snake
that silently feeds itself on the frog.

I am the child in Uganda, all skin and bones,
my legs as thin as bamboo sticks,
And I am the arms merchant,
selling deadly weapons to Uganda.

I am a member of the politburo,
with plenty of power in my hands.
And I am the man who has to pay
his "debt of blood" to my people
dying slowly in a forced labor camp.

My joy is like spring, so warm
it makes flowers bloom all over the Earth.
My pain is like a river of tears,
so vast it fills the four oceans.

Please call me by my true names,
so I can hear all my cries and laughter at once,
so I can see that my joy and pain are one.

Please call me by my true names,
so I can wake up
and the door of my heart
could be left open,
the door of compassion.

So, I make a new plan. I pass out copies of "Please Call Me by My True Names" for everyone to read to themselves. Then I ask them to write about it. After that, everyone stands in a line across the room, placing themselves according to how well they feel they understand the poem. I then invite the individuals at the beginning and end of the line to pair up and step away, continuing this process until everyone has a partner. The person in each pair who feels they don't understand the poem shares with their partner first. Those who feel they understand it are encouraged to listen deeply and take in the fresh response from the "beginner's mind" of their partner.

Listening

Deep listening—a form of open listening with one's heart, without judgment or agenda, reaction or response—is a vital element of the course. I encourage the teachers to take the practice of deep listening back to their homes and schools. In my next newsletter for educators, I report about the Avalokita retreat:

Newsletter #39—Just Listening

In a previous Newsletter I invited listeners to practice listening without comment, without questions, and without gesture or facial expression. The theme of that newsletter was nonjudgment, but just listening *is much more than refraining from positive or negative reactions. To listen deeply, we refrain from analyzing what we hear. Not that there is anything wrong with thinking about what we hear, see, or feel.*

However, mindfulness presupposes a distinction between our direct experience and our commentary on our direct experience. We can see that listening may be as much about ourselves as about our partners. One way to help students develop this focus is to ask them to watch their breath or notice the sensations in their feet without concocting ideas about them. The foot exercise is easier than just listening to a person speak.

Twice during a recent course for Italian teachers, I invited the group to just listen to their partners for five minutes. I was paired with a participant the first time but was an observer the second. The listeners appeared remarkably attentive, yet inexpressive. When I invited the participants to describe their experiences to the whole group, no one volunteered.

Then Loredana, a teacher in a school for teenagers in Palermo, told us that she had found just listening a big challenge. She'd done her best to practice it and, for a brief moment, something completely unexpected happened. As she listened, she vanished. There was no longer a separation between her and her partner. It was as if she were hearing her partner's words while dwelling *inside* the other woman. Loredana later told me she'd had similar experiences at times when listening to her son. This time, knowing no response was expected of her, she felt free, able to stop thinking and just listen. Loredana was inspired. Yes, it is possible to listen deeply to a relative stranger. She pledged to take the practice into her life as a parent, friend, and teacher. She inspired all of us to keep just listening when we returned home.

The warmth, support, and trust I find at Avalokita fires my creativity. I feel more willing to take risks in my teaching. The following week I'm happy to take this expansive spirit with me as I co-teach with Sr. Annabel and Sr. Jewel once again. We enjoy a multilayered and lovely event. However, my most memorable mindfulness experience in Germany is still to come.

Vermont Reflection:
July 27, 2013—Let the Buddha Do It

I cannot begin to count the blessings from these last four weeks.[46] The participants in the weeklong courses for educators at the Avalokita Center in Castelli, Italy, and the European Institute of Applied Buddhism in Waldbröl, Germany, so inspire me with their openness and vulnerability and their sharing of suffering, joy, and love. Each day of these courses, the experience of community deepened. I learned so much from Sr. Annabel and Sr. Jewel, from all the participants, and from my own teaching.

This afternoon I had an unexpected opportunity to practice one of these teachings. Brother Nandiyo had driven me to Cologne Bonn Airport where I planned to catch a Lufthansa flight to Munich and, after a two-hour layover, another Lufthansa flight to Boston. When we arrived at the airport, I discovered that my flight to Munich had been cancelled. The agent immediately rebooked me on an Air Berlin flight. I'd have less than an hour in Munich to catch my flight to Boston. When I arrived at Munich International Airport, the flight to Boston was already boarding in the H section of the international terminal. My shuttle bus drove halfway around the large airport and stopped at the entrance to the H gates. As always in Germany, passengers from curbside boarded using the front door of the bus. But no passengers were allowed to exit at the H gates. I had to wait for the G gates. I finally entered the long G-gate hall at 3:30 p.m. with no boarding pass. I had flown to Munich on Air Berlin, not Lufthansa.

In Italy I had given a Dharma talk that described three practices for letting go: first to accept what is, second to ask, "Am I sure?", and third to stop efforting and turn the job over to Buddha. Standing in that crowded hallway, I had no choice but to let go. Buddha arrived almost immediately, a smiling black man driving a yellow cart. It took him a moment to comprehend the gravity of my situation, and we were off! First stop, the nearest Lufthansa agent to whom my Buddha showed my itinerary. Then up one level on an elevator, where he gave my passport to an officer to get an exit stamp. Then to the front of a long line of people waiting to have their passports checked in order to board Lufthansa's international flights, and on to Gate H44, where my boarding pass was waiting for me. "Welcome, Mr. Brady," the gate agent said. "We knew you were on the way, as Air Berlin notified us they were transferring your luggage to our flight."

Before my Buddha departed, I asked his name. "Alfred," he said. I teared up. That was the name of my German grandfather who had helped many of our Jewish family members leave Germany in the 1930s.

Interbeing

After returning from Germany, I attend Thây's retreat for educators at Brock University in St. Catherines, Ontario. Of the 1,300 participants, 800 are educators. How moving and profound for me to practice mindfulness with so many teachers. Here I meet Katherine Weare, a retired professor of education from England who with Thây coauthored the book *Happy Teachers Change the World*, presenting Thây's practices to educators. I also meet with Sr. Lang Nghiem from Blue Cliff Monastery and John Bell, a Boston Dharma teacher in Thây's tradition. We begin to plan the first US retreat for Applied Ethics, now renamed "Wake Up Schools." After adding Valerie Brown, a friend and gifted retreat leader, to the leadership team, she, John, and I spend hours on the phone planning for the education retreat in July 2014.

As this retreat approaches, I prepare a Dharma talk on interbeing for the first morning. After a bad fall two days before the retreat, I spend the following days recuperating. I will not attend the retreat. Lying there, I sense the energy of people gathering at Blue Cliff and feel confident the retreat will be beautiful and transformative without me. I know with certainty that I don't need to be there in person. I'm present there in the bodies of others.

Avalokita Redux

The following summer I return to Avalokita with more innovations in mind. We wait until the second morning to introduce ourselves and share our gifts. The first evening participants slowly eat one raisin with mindfulness. Then, after I introduce basic mindfulness practices, they get to know a partner by holding the other's hand in silence, a practice I learned in Plum Village twenty-three years earlier.

This new format works well. However, at the opening staff meeting, I make what turns out to be a fateful decision. Stefano asks about Noble Silence. It is scheduled to start every day at the end of the evening program. When should it end? Feeling the collective energy of staff members around me, I suggest Noble Silence end after lunch. From the beginning of the retreat, there are problems. I watch conversations taking place during outdoor walking meditation. I hear a group returning to Avalokita at 10 p.m. finishing their conversations outside the building. There are complaints in Dharma sharing groups about too much Noble Silence. I'm upset. Friends on the staff tell me to relax, that Italians love to talk, teachers most of all. I don't know how to respond to the breakdown of silence, but I'm not ready to accept things as they are.

Vermont Reflection:
August 10, 2015—Let the Sangha Do It

August 7th at 7:15 a.m. Elisabeth picks up her phone in Vermont and hears a chorus of twenty-five voices singing "Happy Birthday" in Italian. Composed mostly of teachers on a weeklong retreat, our group has just concluded an hour and a half Quaker-style Meeting for Business to decide what to do about "the problem" of Noble Silence. Nobody was happy. Many who were new to mindfulness, even a few longtime practitioners, did not understand the value of so much quiet. After all, they could be conversing with interesting new friends. A smaller number, for whom transformation seemed more important than conversation, were upset by talking that frequently intruded on their silence. On the seventh day of the retreat, I gave up and let the Buddha solve our problem. As Thây tells us, the Sangha will be the next incarnation of the Buddha. So, I turned the issue over to everyone as a Sangha.

In the quiet of the meditation hall, everyone shared thoughts on silence. For one, silence had ceased to be a rule and had become a refuge. Another understood the value silence has for others and suggested we create a designated meeting and talking area outside the building. This was a popular proposal, but in the end, it was clear that doing so would divide the Sangha into two groups, much as smoking and nonsmoking teachers' lounges had earlier divided school faculties in Italy. Finally, everyone endorsed a proposal to end Noble Silence after breakfast the next and final day of the retreat.

We listened deeply and spoke from the heart—the feeling of interbeing was profound. Elisabeth hears this in our happy-birthday voices.

I'm invited to return to Avalokita for a third time in July 2016. I decide to make the seven factors of enlightenment our theme. It's an eight-day retreat, with one factor a day for seven days and the final day for Q&A. Stefano sends me a message beforehand: What do I want to do about Noble Silence? I suggest we leave that decision to the retreatants. The first evening I inform the group that "rest" will be the following day's focus.

"Our minds need rest as well as our bodies. When we talk, we don't give our minds a chance to rest. Tomorrow we'll observe Noble Silence through the end of lunch, then enjoy a period of total relaxation in which we'll progressively invite parts of our bodies to relax, beginning with our toes and continuing up to the tops of our heads. Following that, we'll decide how much silence we want to observe for the rest of the retreat."

The next afternoon, the group assembles to seek unity on the question of whether to extend silence through lunch or to end it earlier. The group of sixteen includes five who are entirely new to mindfulness. One woman tells us that since she does not know anyone else there, she needs to talk to make connections. Another says that staying silent even through breakfast is a stretch. A third needs to call her children every morning.

One new practitioner, however, finds this a rare opportunity to explore quietude. She doesn't want to miss it. The experienced practitioners chime in. In the end, the group agrees to observe Noble Silence through lunch with the exception of necessary conversations which can take place outside. The opening day of silence has established a tone. Although not everyone observes the decision entirely, the power of the group's process contributes to a strong retreat and a sense of genuine community.

Other opportunities await me at Wake Up Schools retreats in the US. In June 2022, I join Fern, a former Plum Village monastic, and Elena, a former Wake Up Schools Level II mentee of mine, to offer "The Gift of True Presence," a four-day educators' retreat at Morning Sun Mindfulness Center in nearby New Hampshire. I arrive with a broken humerus near my right shoulder, incurred by a fall onto a rock five days before. By this time, the pain has lost its sharp bite. This is not the case for the deep emotional pain many of the educators are bearing from the deaths of schoolchildren in Uvalde, Texas, a month ago and the fear it has caused in their own schools. In the face of such suffering, it's common for people to shut down, to close their hearts for self-protection. But such wounds must be exposed to air and light to begin to heal.

The following evening, we offer a healing ceremony. We sit in the darkened hall listening to a solo cello and chant to Avalokita to invoke compassion for all who died and all who continue to suffer. We walk slowly, one by one, to the altar to place a small candle and red flower petals representing the blood of the departed young ones. In that safe space created by our community of thirty-five, tears flow. We acknowledge and share the presence of our suffering and our compassion.

The next evening, we have a be-in ceremony with contributions from the ridiculous to the sublime—songs, poetry, stories—gales of laughter one minute, deep listening the next. Our hearts open to communal joy. I've attended many similar tea ceremonies but none with such bliss. For me, these two ceremonies are one, a celebration of all that life can hold.

Educators, like other practitioners, express Plum Village practice in unique ways. This is also the case for their teaching. There is no Plum Village pedagogy. My own approach to teaching mindfulness is experential. I begin by sharing a practice, a reading, or an experience; then provide time to journal and connect with their own experience and mindfully share with another educator or a group. With seeds thus planted, what I then water with my own sharing will already be sending out tender shoots.

In 2019, my aspiration to pass on the teachings I've received from Thầy and other mentors takes a new form. I begin writing *Walking the Teacher's Path with Mindfulness: Stories for Reflection and Action*, recollections of lessons I've received and shared throughout fifty years teaching mathematics and Dharma. I'm especially grateful for this new focus when the pandemic puts an end to in-person educator retreats. I'm doubly grateful when Stefano creates a remote mindfulness course for Italian, Francophone, and Anglophone educators, which Kaira Jewel Lingo, formerly Sr. Jewel, and I co-teach. We teach mindfulness for Italian educators again in 2021 with John Bell.

When Thầy teaches about interbeing, he often points out that a flower is made entirely of non-flower elements—the sun, the rain, the earth, and ultimately, the entire cosmos. As I teach mindfulness, I am aware of the non-Richard elements in me. I feel united with teachers, mentors, family, and friends who had once seemed distinct from "Richard." Most of all, I feel the presence of Thầy within me.

Reflection—Bodhicitta

The seed of bodhicitta can be found in everyone's store consciousness, but it may have atrophied from lack of use or nourishment. I've noticed my own seed growing in spurts, responding to particular people or occasions, many described in these pages. A deeper explanation given by Quaker economist Kenneth Boulding now seems closer to the truth.[47] He posits that consciousness is always absorbing information at some level. However, information that conflicts with beliefs or prior knowledge is likely to bypass awareness unless it's particularly powerful or confirms a critical level of previously stored material in the unconscious. Then transformation can occur. Thầy's terminology would be something like *ongoing change in store consciousness can become sufficient for one additional cause to initiate transformation at the level of awareness.* This was what seemed to happen when, after reading Leslie Rawls' article, I brought my childhood loneliness *into* my meditation and could finally receive the Great Mother's embrace. I feel the same about meeting Thầy. Long before I was aware of it, nourishing bodhicitta in students and teachers had become my life's work. Thầy was inspirational in helping me realize this—and in so many other ways.

When I was confronted by the problem of Noble Silence at Avalokita, I realized that a true resolution would require participants to change. Some years earlier, Ronald Heifetz's book *Leadership without Easy Answers* offered me insights into solutions that required what Heifetz called "adaptive change."[48] Heifetz posits that a situation must be ripe before this kind of change can take place. Turning the resolution over to the community created an interbeing experience that evoked bodhicitta and accomplished that ripening. Years earlier I'd thought that few ninth grade Sidwell Friends students, despite being aware of their stress, would be drawn to mindfulness as an antidote. Giving them a five-minute window allowed them to see their stress in bold relief and discover a new way to relate to themselves through mindfulness meditation.

Nourishing bodhicitta in math classes, which are based on analytical thinking, was a challenge for me. Devoting the first five minutes of each class to contemplative practice seemed to resonate for many of the students. In a course evaluation, one tenth grader wrote: "I have learned great things from myself in the way that I respond to quotes in my journal and in how I respond to myself in free writing. In writing continuously, I often write things that I did not understand consciously before they hit the paper."

And another, commenting on her previous response to a commencement address by Steve Jobs: "I began to think that maybe it was not so bad to be clueless (about life direction); I am not as restricted by my own thoughts, and on the contrary, am quite free to explore and try to find something that I really do love."

Day after day these students shared their bodhicitta in small groups. The "interbeing nature" of our classroom Sangha took its course as a river does, creating an enjoyable and focused atmosphere described by one student as "just the way it should be, an optimum learning environment."

Invitation

Sit in a comfortable position. Relax. Let your eyes close and breathe in and out slowly three times. Invite your life into your awareness. Notice whatever experiences, feelings, or thoughts about bodhicitta, your awakened nature, the mind of love, come to mind. Notice the place of bodhicitta in your life activities and decisions. When you feel ready, open your eyes.

PART SIX

DOING AND BEING

One day in New York City I met a Buddhist scholar and I told her about my practice of mindfulness in the vegetable garden. I enjoy growing lettuce, tomatoes, and other vegetables and I like to spend time gardening every day. She said, "You shouldn't spend your time growing vegetables. You should spend more time writing poems. Your poems are so beautiful. Everyone can grow lettuce, but not everyone can write poems like you do." I told her, "If I don't grow lettuce, I can't write poems."

When I'm taking care of the lettuce or watering my garden I don't think of poetry or writing. I focus my mind entirely on taking care of the lettuce, watering the vegetables and so on. I enjoy every moment and I do it in a mode of "non-thinking." It's very helpful to stop the thinking. Your art is conceived in the depths of your consciousness while you're not thinking about it. The moment when you express it is only a moment of birth, the moment you deliver the baby. For me, there must be moments when you allow the child inside you to grow, so you can do your best and your masterpiece can contain insight, understanding, and compassion.

—Thich Nhat Hanh,
Answers from the Heart

Fifteenth-century Indian mystic poet Kabir beautifully contrasts doing and being:

BREATH

Are you looking for me? I am in the next seat.

My shoulder is against yours.

You will not find me in stupas, not in Indian shrine rooms,

nor in synagogues, nor in cathedrals:

not in masses, nor in kirtans, not in legs winding around your

own neck, nor in eating nothing but vegetables.

When you really look for me, you will see me instantly—

you will find me in the tiniest house of time.

Kabir says: Student, tell me what is God?

He is the breath inside the breath.[49]

This poem embodies the Buddha's teaching on Right Mindfulness, an element of the Noble Eightfold Path. Thây emphasizes the essential role of *presence* in practicing the Four Foundations of Mindfulness: mindfulness of the body *in* the body, mindfulness of the feelings *in* the feelings, mindfulness of mind *in* the mind, and mindfulness of the objects of mind *in* the objects of mind.[50] In Thây's response to the scholar, above, when he engages in gardening as a spiritual practice, he's one with the act of watering and one with the lettuce. There's no separation between Thây and the lettuce, there is *just watering*. This present moment awareness which Kabir calls "God," is the "breath inside the breath."

Most of us are *doing* something when we water lettuce. We're watering the lettuce and thinking about what we're doing or thinking about something else. This thinking is a form of doing. It also happens when we meditate on the breath. We feel it as *our* breath, an object of mind separate from ourselves. If we stop thinking, breathing remains—not the breath we're observing that is separate from the observer, not we who are doing the observing, only "the breath inside the breath." True *being* is interbeing. When we live this way, without separation, any form of action—thought, speech, or bodily action—is *being*.

As a thinker, a speaker, or an actor, we are inevitably a doer. Thầy often refers to our NST—nonstop thinking—as a way we avoid feeling our inner suffering. Until we can *be* with suffering and happiness, with whatever the present moment holds, manas consciousness will push it away or grasp it. Our practice can begin with samatha—stopping and calming—and continue with vipassana—looking deeply—or with deep listening, compassion, or any other interbeing practice.

Life requires doing. Insight and peace require being. Thầy helps us begin to let go of nonstop doing and step into being.

Chapter 13

COMMENCEMENT

There are many things we are unable to leave behind, which trap us. Practice looking deeply into these things. In the beginning, you may think that they are vital to your happiness, but they may actually be obstacles to your true happiness, causing you to suffer. If you are not able to be happy because you are caught by them, leaving them behind will be a source of joy for you. The Buddha and many of his disciples experienced this, and have handed down their wisdom to us. Please look at the things you think are necessary to your well-being and happiness, and find out whether they bring you happiness or are almost killing you.

—Thich Nhat Hanh,
The Path of Emancipation

Retirement

As the end of the 2005–2006 school year approaches, I reflect on the ways this has been the most satisfying year of my teaching career. Perhaps another exciting year lies ahead, one that will benefit from all that I've learned from this year's Math II experience. I feel a larger calling from the new mindfulness-in-education movement. Irene and I want to compile a book of stories from teachers who have attended our workshops about where they've taken mindfulness in their classrooms. I want to share mindfulness at other schools, to be available to go when called. My teaching schedule feels binding to me now, and I tell School Head Bruce Stewart that the coming year will be my last. Along with my excitement, I also contemplate the anticipated loss. Retiring after thirty-seven years of teaching will be a huge life change. I'll need support. I invite four friends to meet with me regularly to help me prepare for retirement and whatever comes next.

Several years earlier, Elisabeth expressed her reservations about continuing to live in Takoma Park, Maryland. She wanted a simpler, more rural life and began visiting cohousing communities that might be a good fit for our retirement. Although I visit some of them with her, I can't see myself leaving the DC area. After she begins to search in Vermont near Shoshanna's college, a friend points us toward a new cohousing project in rural Putney, which we investigate. Putney, it turns out, is not only near Shoshanna's college, but also the home of a vibrant Quaker meeting.

It's hard for me to contemplate this move. I'm comfortable with business as usual. Elisabeth grew up on a farm and in a small town. I've always been a city boy: Chicago, Boston, DC. I've now lived in the DC area for forty years, taught at Sidwell Friends for thirty-three, and been part of the Washington Mindfulness Community for seventeen. Before me lies the unknown. My support group listens attentively to my plans and reports of school visits, workshops, conferences, and the book editing project with Irene. They sit quietly and breathe with me. I phone Paula: "Richard, you can't know what lies ahead," she says, "but you can trust that everything you've done in your life so far has prepared you."

Farewell

At an upper school assembly, the day before graduation, I bid farewell to departing seniors with William Glasser's words: "There are only two places in the world where time takes precedence over the job to be done. School and prison."[51] This leads me to the question, "What is 'the job to be done'?" I'd found an answer to that question several years earlier in *Parent/Teen Breakthrough: The Relationship Approach*. Co-authors Mira Kirshenbaum and Charles Foster write: "Teens have only two jobs to do: to figure out who they are and to leave home."[52]

"During my thirty-four years at Sidwell Friends," I continue, "I've worked with a number of people who knew who they were, and I was inspired to look within and understand myself more deeply. However long you've been at our school, I hope you too have found models you wish to emulate." I reflect on the more than one thousand Meetings for Worship I've attended, hours that have played a vital role in getting to know myself.

"Have you been able to learn faster than I did? I hope so. As for leaving home, home is ideally a place where unconditional acceptance and love are bestowed in full measure. How wonderful if all of you can go on to new places where you'll receive unconditional acceptance and love. Sidwell Friends tries to help you make a home inside yourself. In Meeting for Worship, you've stood before five hundred peers and faculty members and apologized to friends, shared losses and fears without embarrassment or excuse, and revealed to all of us the power of acceptance and love."

I conclude with a short meditation:

> Breathing in, I am aware of myself.
> Breathing out, I am home.

Anxiety

While moving smoothly through the outward forms of closure, I'm not in a mood to celebrate. Tears are near the surface—feelings of doubt, loneliness, and fear about the future. Will I be able to take *home* with me to Vermont where I've agreed to move with Elisabeth after I retire? Will I be moving inexorably toward death while Elisabeth moves toward life, the rural life she loves? In Vermont, she will once again enjoy the simple life. Shoshanna will be near us, but I have no friends there. I have no Buddhist community and no contacts with people engaged with mindfulness in education. In this first rural area for me, will there be access to the jazz, films, and ethnic food I love? I feel lost. I need to pay careful attention. Reality is less threatening than the swirling stories in my mind. Dropping beneath the stories and the emotions, I locate emptiness. In that emptiness is a connection to the present moment that I record in my journal several days later.

Journal entry—June 18, 2007

I've had a "retirement" celebration and written my last student comment. Now that there are no more lessons to plan, grades to give, or comments to write; a space opens. I fill it by reading the transcription of a talk sent by a friend. As soon as I start to read, the new space closes again, and I'm back in that all too familiar "doing" mode. There are always plenty of things to do. I could be doing some of them now. But I choose to write and soon, more importantly, to stop writing—to sit and to feel.

Impermanence is a fundamental Buddhist teaching. It's the third of the Three Marks of Existence and the fourth of the Five Remembrances [Appendix 5] that Plum Village monastics recite daily: "All that I hold dear and everyone I love is of the nature to change. There is no way to escape being separated from them." I haven't been reciting this. I suspect things would feel different if I did.

I share my growing apprehension with my support group. Moving to the country on top of leaving friends, spiritual community, and job feels staggering. Will our proximity to Shoshanna be a sufficient anchor for my new life? As summer progresses, I feel increasingly apprehensive. Fall arrives. Students return to school, and I don't. I no longer have the safety net of a teacher's identity or a teacher's schedule to order my day. I no longer absorb the wild and wonderful energy of hundreds of adolescents. My anxiety turns to sadness, and then to depression. Vigor has evaporated from my life, but I think I know where I can find it again. In November, I leave for a stay in Plum Village, returning home after a month much restored but still anxious.

Chapter 14

THIS IS IT

Every one of us is trying to find our true home. Some of us are still searching. Our true home is inside, but it's also in our loved ones around us. When you're in a loving relationship, you and the other person can be a true home for each other.

—Thich Nhat Hanh,
How to Love

Vermont

We move to Vermont the following July. When we first arrive, I'm not able to see the conditions for happiness. The quiet beauty of the countryside is no substitute for old friends and city life. How do I make sense of my new life? This place is foreign to me. Out of this big question, I begin writing "Vermont Reflections." The Washington Mindfulness Community asked me to stay in touch, so I send them my first Vermont Reflection. I then decide to send it out more widely. I don't revel in my new life, but through writing about it I'm able to approach it with curiosity, wondering what it has to teach me. My idleness becomes a plus. There is ample time to observe, reflect, and write. I journal weekly reflections on my life in Vermont for the first year and a half, and two hundred entries over the next eight years. I don't just share what's happening. I digest my experiences, chew on them as if they were challenging math problems that

I return to again and again with new thoughts. Journaling this way sometimes leads to fresh insights or a deeper understanding of an old lesson. Writing becomes a spiritual practice.

Vermont Reflection:
July 14, 2008—I have arrived. I am home.

Departing from the Hanoi airport last May, I talked with a Zen priest from Australia named "Enlightened Compassion." I'd been on retreat with him for three weeks, but this was our first conversation. I began by asking if he was looking forward to going home. "I am home," he replied.

His response has been very much with me lately during my first days in Vermont. With Shoshanna living in Takoma Park for the summer, we are temporary guests in her Brattleboro apartment, awaiting the completion of our home in Putney this fall.

Having arrived late Wednesday evening, I awaken the next morning sobbing, lonely, a stranger in a strange land. What am I doing here? I'm disoriented. I don't know who I am. Only one of the close relationships through which I've anchored myself is here—Elisabeth. From our landing I can see the New Hampshire mountains, but we're not on vacation. This Brattleboro home is confusing. But face it I must. This is my here and now.

Almost immediately events begin to coalesce. In the morning we visit our new home, still under construction. More shock. Will we really be living here? We attend a meeting of the Putney Commons cohousing group in one of the already completed homes. Following afternoon naps, we spend two hours as volunteers bagging groceries at the Brattleboro Food Co-op, then stay on for dinner.

Twenty minutes after we sit down in the dining area of the Co-op, Jon, an educator and fellow student of Thich Nhat Hanh, appears: "Richard, I can't believe this. I was just talking about you with my massage therapist. She's looking for a Thich Nhat Hanh sitting group. I was telling her that a Dharma teacher in that tradition would be moving to Putney soon. Here you are!"

By Friday morning I've met her, and we've set up a meeting and meditation at her office for the next Tuesday evening. I've also received a haircut from David, who I hope will replace Diego, my DC barber of forty-two years. Later in the afternoon our DC friend Bill arrives for a visit and to attend a day of mindfulness in Connecticut with Elisabeth and me. I have arrived. I'm beginning to feel at home.

The theme of the day of mindfulness turns out to be the Buddha's Sutra on the Full Awareness of Breathing.[53] Bert Mayo gives the Dharma talk, first covering various schools of Zen and mentioning koan practice. Bert shares two well-known ones: "Who am I?" and "What is this?" Then he explains the background of the sutra and comments on its sixteen parts. I'm engaged. Later Tom Duva and Mike Geres lead us in an extended guided meditation using each part of the discourse as a focus. The last two invitations are to breathe in and out, aware of the cessation of notions, then to breathe in and out and let go. As I start the cessation of notions, the words of the monk Enlightened Compassion come back to me. "I am home." For him, the here and now is always home.

On Thursday morning Brattleboro and Shoshanna's apartment had not been home. By Friday evening they have begun to feel a bit more familiar. New relationships and interconnections are taking shape: a house, a living community, friends, a Sangha, even a barber. This new security allows me to begin to feel at home. I recall the Buddha inviting me to discard old clothes and stand naked in the here and now, responding to the koan "Who am I?" with "Just this."

No Coming, No Going

Elisabeth and I aren't prepared to cut our ties with Takoma Park. Instead of selling our house there, we rent it out, setting aside the loft to use when we're in town and leaving one car there. DC is such a deep part of who I am. After moving to Vermont, I take the train south once a month to visit friends and attend WMC sittings. At them we often sing "No Coming, No Going" when someone is about to move away or when a friend or relative has died:

No coming, no going.
No after, no before.
I hold you close to me.
I release you to be so free
because I am in you
and you are in me.[54]

This song inspires a talk I offer to the Washington Mindfulness Community about life transitions. Three years later, this song strengthens my practice of interbeing on my visits to support my best friend Bob as his cancer progresses. Although not a brother by blood, Bob Burton, my lifelong friend and former MIT bridge partner, is truly a brother. In the years since college, I was the frequent recipient of Bob's wisdom on navigating life at home and at work. After taking up mindfulness practice, I had wisdom to share with him. Near the end of his life, Bob offers me a remarkable lesson on impermanence:

For many years, scuba diving was my favorite activity. Once a friend asked me whether there was an aspect of diving that stood out for me. "Finding and swimming with sharks," I replied immediately. When my friend asked why, I couldn't say. But now that I've survived esophageal cancer, I know why. Swimming with sharks and living on the edge of death both forced me to be completely in the moment. There was no future, only the present.

Bob's story resonates with me. Like Bob, experiences in my life stood out for reasons I couldn't explain at the time. Nevertheless, they watered and strengthened seeds in my store consciousness readying them to sprout into my awareness as conditions changed.

After moving to Vermont, I travel to Washington to visit Bob several times. When Elisabeth is unable to accompany me to his memorial service, my WMC sister Susan Hadler invites me to stay with her, and her husband and accompanies me to the memorial. Eight years later, Susan has moved to Madison, Wisconsin, where she contracts encephalitis. When I visit her, she has emerged from a coma but is only able to move her feet and arms and turn her head. Her eyes are bright and connecting. Gallantly fighting to come back from the abyss, she whispers a few words. Within days, pneumonia claims her life. Susan and Bob continue to dwell in the Sangha of my heart.

Letting Go

Back in Maryland sorting through a lifetime's accumulation of papers, books, pictures, furniture, and stuff, I see how naturally I look to these things for a sense of identity, a sense of belonging. I see twelve years of my life encapsulated in three diplomas, my connection to my businessman father in his postal scale. Thinking about the process of letting go as I drift off to sleep, I recall a passage from *Look Homeward Angel*:

> *A stone, a leaf, an unfound door; of a stone, a leaf, a door. And of all the forgotten faces. Naked and alone we came into exile. In her dark womb we did not know our mother's face; from the prison of her flesh we come into the unspeakable and incommunicable prison of this earth. Which of us has known his brother? Which of us has looked into his father's heart? Which of us has not remained forever prison-pent? Which of us is not forever a stranger and alone? O waste of loss, in the hot mazes, lost, among bright stars on this most weary unbright cinder, lost! Remembering speechlessly we seek the great forgotten language, the lost lane-end into heaven, a stone, a leaf, an unfound door. Where? When? O lost, and by the wind grieved, ghost, come back again.*[55]

Forty-eight years ago, I wrote my eleventh-grade theme on Thomas Wolfe. I found his writing compelling for reasons I couldn't have understood at the time. As I prune my material connections to the past, I feel a "naked and alone" twinge. However, when I check in with myself, my past is in who I am today—people I haven't seen in years, events long forgotten. The prison Wolfe describes is his illusion of having a separate self. My separate self holds on to records of accomplishments, old letters, and possessions, because they give me a sense of security. These things with solidity and permanence confirm my sense of solidity and permanence.

I see Wolfe's "great forgotten language" as the understanding of impermanence and nonself I was later introduced to in Whitman's "I am large, I contain multitudes" from his "Song for Myself."[56] Whatever I take with me to Vermont are mementos that remind me of people and times that helped shape my life. They are all already a part of me, like departed ancestors, present-day relatives and friends, Shoshanna, and countless students through whom I see myself continuing into future generations.

A work of calligraphy by Thich Nhat Hanh hangs in my room in Vermont reading: "You are life without boundaries." The journey of arriving at this consciousness starting from being "naked and alone" is my life's miraculous work.

Mountains and Rivers

It's been almost twenty years since a small group of us who attended Thầy's early East Coast retreats established the Washington Mindfulness Community. At the time, DC had no other Western-led Sanghas. By the time we arrive in Brattleboro in 2008, we find the Vermont Insight Meditation Center and Tibetan Buddhist Sanghas thriving in the area. Will there be interest in a new Sangha in the Plum Village tradition?

Whenever I attended one of Thây's retreats, I felt blessed to have a Sangha at home to return to. This wasn't true for many participants, particularly in the 1990s. Optional retreat sessions on creating a Sangha became important. I enjoyed facilitating. A group from the same area who met at a retreat, as we had, found it much easier going home and starting a Sangha together than it would've been if they hadn't met there. In those early years, "mindfulness" had little media attention and only a few Vietnam-era peace activists were familiar with Thich Nhat Hanh. Since Sanghas would be unfamiliar to people back home, I proposed first offering a study/practice group using *Beginning Mindfulness: Learning the Way of Awareness, A Ten-Week Course* by Andrew Weiss, an early student of Thây's and advertising the group in bookstores, coffee shops, and alternative health venues. Such a group might naturally morph into a Sangha at the conclusion of its study.

In 2008, following our move to Vermont, Elisabeth and I follow the advice I'd given to so many others to found a Sangha. We begin, as we did in DC, with a study class, but not all that many people enroll. Vermont winter weather, travel, and other commitments make for irregular attendance. Departing from Andrew's format, Elisabeth adds singing and qigong. She also offers a session on gatha writing, and I contribute an exercise in mindful speech and deep listening.

The week following the last class in the series, we invite participants to a tea ceremony and oracle reading. Each person in the circle asks a question of "the oracle," then picks a small scroll of paper from a bell with several lines of Thây's poetry.

The ceremony and reading are profound. Almost all the students come, along with two friends visiting from New York and three first-time townspeople. Most ask deeply personal questions of the oracle and receive satisfying answers. My question is, "Where do I find happiness?" The verse I draw provides a crystal-clear answer:

I am aware that I owe so much
to my parents, teachers, friends, and all beings.

The tea ceremony is beautiful. We share sources of our joy. One person shows a photo of a beloved dog and another a dress knitted for a Barbie doll. At the end of the evening, one newcomer, who has previously meditated alone, expresses deep appreciation for the love and joy in this community.

The next week we meet as a Sangha. We post flyers around town. At the top is a lovely color photo of Thầy smiling broadly and the words "GOT SMILES!" Beneath are the details of our two sitting groups. Elisabeth facilitates the Brattleboro group, and I lead the one in Putney. Compared to the Washington Mindfulness Community, both groups are quite small. Also, unlike the WMC, which has been around for twenty-five years, other than Elisabeth and me, there are no seasoned practitioners. Over time our Sangha members begin attending retreats at Thầy's Blue Cliff Monastery in upstate New York and daylong sessions sponsored by other Sanghas in our region. We're happy to have friends in the practice in our new home.

Qigong

We've lived in Vermont just a year when I develop a raft of physical symptoms ranging from pain in my right shoulder, fatigue, and night sweats to a twenty-five-pound weight loss. In Thich Nhat Hanh's teaching, body and mind *inter-are*, so it isn't a surprise that I have physical as well as psychological reactions to moving.

Maureen, my first acupuncturist in the 1970s, had been a nurse in Vietnam, where she sustained a back injury that Western medicine couldn't heal. When acupuncture succeeded, she studied it and became a practitioner. She told me her nursing background helped her observe symptoms and pulses to determine whether acupuncture or Western medicine was appropriate, case by case. Maureen's words come back to me in 2009, when my medical condition has no clear Western diagnosis. At Dartmouth-Hitchcock Medical Center, blood tests show an infection, but further tests for specific causes, like Lyme disease, are negative. My new acupuncturist diagnoses my difficulty as retaining *yin* energy, associated with shadows (in Jungian psychology, our darker self) and femininity. She begins treating me with needles and Chinese herbs. I add Indian herbs for joint pain at the recommendation of a friend and receive Jin Shin Jyutsu, an ancient oriental art revived in the early 1900s for harmonizing life energy. Most importantly, I rest.

In Western medicine, symptoms are treated with drugs, surgery, and other approaches to remove symptoms or, sometimes, their root causes. While they may be necessary at times, Western approaches fail to draw on the body's own capacity for healing. In the East, there's an understanding that with sufficient support, over time the body can return to balance. Acupuncture offers feedback to various bodily systems and provides guidance as to what retuning is needed. Herbs strengthen multiple systems. Energy work strengthens resilience.

Healing arrives slowly—more range of motion in my right arm, some increased movement with little or no pain, less intense night sweats, a bit more energy. But I'm impatient. I want to know what's causing the problems with my yin energy. Is there a Western mode that would help? I return for more tests and a referral to a pathologist. It takes Western doctors ten months to identify the cause of my symptoms as psoriatic arthritis, an autoimmune disorder. After the first drug prescribed proves ineffective, I'm placed on a low dose of a strong chemotherapy drug. As blood tests continue to show the presence of extremely high levels of inflammation, I discontinue all Western medicine. A shoulder specialist looks at my MRI and recommends I have my right shoulder replaced.

My acupuncturist tells me my inner energy is completely defended against the outside world, rendering ineffective the Western prescriptions for arthritis. She introduces me to qigong as a way of promoting physical, emotional, and energetic wellness. The first of my two qigong practices circulates *qi* energy around the body. Once this has been done, the second gathers energy from the universe, brings it in, then releases it back to the universe—just what's needed to soften energetic defenses. As I practice, I listen to a recording of Plum Village monastics chanting to bodhisattva Avalokiteshvara for compassion for themselves, for those close to them, and for suffering around the world. Their chanting and the music resonate in me and amplify the healing I receive from the qigong.

Around this time Elisabeth and I see the movie *The King's Speech*. A particular moment about halfway through the film jumps out at me. Prince Albert ("Bertie") has returned to his speech therapist, Lionel. He tells Lionel that he's practicing his speech exercises an hour a day, the same length of time I practice qigong. Bertie struggles to overcome his stammer. Doing qigong, the arthritic pains in my arms set up a struggle of a different sort. Both the king and I wish to move in the direction of ease. There is no instant fix. Now as I practice qigong, I often see an image of Bertie singing, cussing, and struggling through whatever makes his speech come easier.

Qigong is not the same as sitting and walking meditation. Both are skillful ways of developing mindfulness which support qigong practice, but I don't come to them with the back-against-the-wall gravity I bring to qigong. Once Prince Albert comes to believe in his teacher Lionel, he accepts his methods and practices them. There's no other path open to him. I have a similar belief in the long-term effectiveness of qigong. However, with the cold weather and the spread of the condition to my left shoulder and arm, I'm unclear as to how far qigong will take me. My situation also differs from Albert's in that there are options available to me from Western medicine. I'll receive cortisone injections in both shoulders next Tuesday. Some years ago, for arthritis in my knee, a cortisone injection reduced the inflammation. It never returned. If these injections don't produce similar results, I face the possibility of a shoulder replacement.

I start to accept this moment with all its uncertainty. With this acceptance comes freedom. Perhaps this evening I'll find more ease in qigong. Perhaps not.

After two years of Eastern treatments and practice, I reach a point where I rarely experience arthritic pain. I feel stronger, freer. Friends who haven't seen me in a while tell me how different, how much healthier I look. Eventually I go for acupuncture less often but continue qigong. I am ready to engage in new opportunities.

Chapter 15

THẦY

Bhikkhus, the teaching is merely a vehicle to describe the truth. Don't mistake it for the truth itself. A finger pointing at the moon is not the moon. The finger is needed to know where to look for the moon, but if you mistake the finger for the moon itself, you will never know the real moon. The teaching is like a raft that carries you to the other shore. The raft is needed, but the raft is not the other shore. An intelligent person would not carry the raft around on his head after making it across to the other shore. Bhikkhus, my teaching is the raft which can help you cross to the other shore beyond birth and death. Use the raft to cross to the other shore, but don't hang onto it as your property. Do not become caught in the teaching. You must be able to let it go.

—Thich Nhat Hanh,
Old Path, White Clouds: Walking in the Footsteps of the Buddha

Plum Village 2014

In 2014 Thầy will turn eighty-eight. Every opportunity to be near him is precious, especially during his twenty-one-day retreat at Plum Village in June on the topic "What Happens When We're Alive? What Happens When We Die?"[57] During an earlier retreat Thầy related a story of an interview with a journalist who asked what he hoped to do before he died.

"I told the journalist I'm doing now what I want to do before I die. I didn't think saying that I won't die would be understood." He continues, "As I look around the meditation hall, I see my continuation in each one of you." We are a part of Thây's "continuation body," as is everyone whose lives he, his teaching—all his actions—have touched directly or indirectly. I know this retreat will be a deep one.

In the first days of the retreat, I dream that all 700 lay retreatants and 200 monastics are on a ship, and Thây is our captain. We're headed for the shore of liberation. During the twenty-one days of the actual retreat voyage, I frequently connect in heartfelt ways with old and new friends. As the voyage progresses, many of us shed our everyday awareness for an extraordinarily profound consciousness.

During a sharing of my Dharma family group, named "Wisteria," my Austrian friend Arnold tells us about the prior day's Jewish/German dialogue. "Why weren't you there, Richard?" he asks. Sitting in silence with Arnold's question, I touch the suffering of my German-Jewish ancestors—suffering I haven't touched in the twenty years since my visit to the Holocaust Museum with Gabriela. My father never seemed to feel this pain, much less to transform it. That work was bequeathed to me. With tears in my eyes, I share how overwhelmed I feel.

My father's family and their cousins were fortunate—fortunate to be living in the north of Germany where anti-Semitism was slower to take hold, fortunate to have financial means, fortunate that my grandfather saw trouble coming in 1935 and set an example for the rest of the family by emigrating to the US with his wife, children, and brothers the following year. Everyone else followed his lead, finding new homes in the US, Palestine, England, South Africa, Chile, and Australia. My father never talked about what he left behind, but the story is a core part of my heritage. Now it's time for me to listen. I tell Arnold I will attend the next Jewish/German dialogue if he's at my side for support.

At the end of the first week, I make another choice. I've been devoting a lot of energy to connecting with others. I'm happily renewing old friendships and forging new ones in our close-knit Wisteria family and beyond. Do I continue making connections a priority, or shall I focus more energy on my personal suffering, suffering that is getting perilously close to the surface? I recall my first time in Plum Village, in June 1992—Thầy telling us the most important reason to be here is to be part of the Sangha. Two friends I met back then are here at this retreat twenty-two years later. Others I met at later retreats at Plum Village and in the US, Vietnam, and Germany are here now, as are Sister Pine and Sister Peace who were members of my root Sangha in Washington. This is a precious time to immerse myself in Sangha practice. There will be plenty of time to focus on suffering when I get home. But it's really not up to me, is it? As it turns out, suffering and I are about to come face-to-face.

Practicing with Suffering

I'm looking forward to a Lazy Day gathering with educators from Asia. I've been invited to give a keynote talk at a conference in Hong Kong the next year. I hope this opportunity will help me prepare. Twenty- five of us arrive at the Upper Hamlet Transformation Hall. In the middle of our space, we find three prone bodies. We sit quietly and wait for them to leave. Indistinguishable words flow from a nearby CD player. We're ready to begin our sharing when I hear David, the organizer, ask someone to gently rouse the prone guests. I don't notice what happens next, but following their departure, David asks us to take a few moments to send them positive energy.

Five hours later I've just washed my lunch dishes when two of the three retreatants who were asked to leave the Transformation Hall approach me. Henri and Celeste are a French couple. Henri is incensed. "You're the one responsible for the group and you're a Dharma teacher. You understand what interbeing means, yet you interrupted our meditation when we were almost finished!" Henri goes on this way for some time. I listen, breathe, and embrace him with the compassion of my heart. When he pauses, I apologize on behalf of our group. "I'm so sorry. I understand why you're upset. I'll convey your unhappiness to the organizer of the meeting when I see him." Henri calms down, and I bow to him and to Celeste.

The next day near the end of outdoor walking meditation, the sound of a bell invites us to stop, breathe, and enjoy our surroundings. I turn around to see Henri and Celeste a few feet away. Without hesitating, I approach Henri, look him in the eye and say, "You are more beautiful today than you were yesterday." He smiles, and we bow to each other.

On the final morning of the retreat, as I prepare a sandwich to take with me, I spy the two of them at the other end of the dining room. They approach me. Without words, Henri bows and we hug mindfully.

Culmination

The Buddha, the Dharma, and the Sangha inter-are. The energy of Thầy's poignant talks penetrates and enriches our interactions. Even in difficult encounters, I feel my heart embracing interbeing. Our Wisteria Dharma family calls two extra meetings to share our understanding of Thầy's talks. Toward the end of the retreat, with gratitude and tears, I attend a morning of Jewish/German dialogue with Arnold. No words come. Just hearing the pain of others who continue to bear suffering and guilt from the Holocaust is huge.

After the retreat, as I watch the DVDs of Thầy's Dharma talks, I relive the transmission I received during them. While I haven't reached the shore of liberation, it is in sight. I've changed, opened, allowed myself to become more vulnerable. I take more risks. I understand more about myself and others. The only way I can even begin to repay all the gifts I've received is through sharing them with others.

Transmission

A few months later, on November 11, 2014, Thầy suffers a massive stroke. After some months in a Bordeaux hospital, he is transferred to San Francisco for further treatment. Elisabeth and I have planned a family vacation in California over Christmas. A few weeks before we leave, a Dharma teacher friend writes to say she's recently visited Thầy in San Francisco. He is working hard on recovery and welcomes visits from old students. I contact Brother Phap Linh, the monk coordinating Thầy's schedule, and arrange a visit for the two of us.

Our friend Terry generously drives us to one of the beautiful homes in San Francisco's Pacific Heights neighborhood placed at Thầy's disposal. After a short wait in the sisters' residence, we're led through the courtyard to the second home where Thầy and the brothers are staying. We're invited to wait in a large parlor and are soon joined by Sister Chan Không, the monastic closest to our teacher. She describes Thầy's daily life, his therapy, and his progress and shares her hope that Thầy might be able to regain his speech before returning to Plum Village.

A monastic comes in and invites us to join Thầy for lunch. We find him in his wheelchair about to be wheeled to his place at the table. A number of monastic attendants are also present. When I last saw Thầy in June, his energy overflowed. He seemed to dance above the floor as he moved between his cushion and the whiteboard to share visual elements of his teaching. I stand before him now. He's so physically diminished! I collect myself, bow, and look into his eyes, into the depths of my amazing teacher. I can feel his life, his experience, all his good work conveyed in his silent gaze. I sit next to him and do my best to eat in mindfulness. Elisabeth tells me later that as Thầy ate, he repeatedly looked over at me. I overflow with gratitude and love.

As we continue our trip, I often feel Thầy's presence within me. I sense his blessing will in some way guide the rest of my life. Our travels end in Colorado where we are with some of Elisabeth's family. There I awaken from a dream of a phone call from Plum Village. In my dream, a succession of monastics lined up in alphabetical order sing a Plum Village practice song. I think I've heard them all when I suddenly recognize Thây's distinct voice. How could this be? He's still in San Francisco. Two hours later I check my email and find the latest update on Thây: "We are very happy to announce that Thây arrived safely at Bergerac Airport in France this afternoon (Friday, the 8th of January) and returned to his hermitage in Plum Village to a warm welcome of songs and smiles from his monastic disciples." I heard them sing in my dreams!

Tears

I return to Plum Village the following June, joining with many of Thây's longtime students, together for the first time since his stroke. This is more than a family reunion. Our roles have changed. The monastic planning team lays out a series of talks intended to review Thây's basic teachings. Many of us are asked to join the monks and nuns in offering Dharma these talks and presentations. I've heard most of these teachings before from Thây, but now they're repeated by many voices and illustrated with new stories—a fresh Plum Village richness.

One afternoon I'm invited to join Br. Phap Linh in welcoming newcomers to the second half of the retreat the following morning. That evening I request support from my Dharma family. One friend asks what I plan to say. I have no idea, but in that moment, I recall the personal suffering expressed by members of our family and I spontaneously reply, "The end of suffering and happiness ... but not necessarily in that order." In my talk the next morning, I share a dream from the previous day: I'm looking out a window of my family home. I see my father apparently dozing on the porch. In the next moment, he looks at me, his eyes shining with love. I tell the gathering of my joy on awakening from that dream, then ask them to form pairs and share happy times from their own lives.

Nurturing happiness is an important part of Thầy's teaching. That happiness and joy are both born of suffering is expressed in the phrase, "No mud, no lotus." It takes a few weeks before I can see the mud from which my beautiful dream grew. I see that my father's look of love reflected his deepest feeling for me. But here is the mud: He was never able to express his love directly. Thầy is the father who has beamed out his love to all of us. We are all his spiritual children.

While in Plum Village, because of Thầy's stroke I'm caught up in a new sense of responsibility. Many of the old-timers feel the weight of a new kind of leadership. Without Thầy's guidance, what lies ahead? We appreciate the monastics' Herculean job of planning, organizing, and running the retreat. What a gift it is to teach with them. We talk about how smoothly the retreat is going and what the future might hold. But we never talk about losing Thầy in the form we've known him.

A year and a half before, when we received news of his stroke, we cried. Our Sanghas around the world poured out their love and healing energy. This June, many of us gathered at our spiritual home, Plum Village. We saw our beloved teacher silent in his wheelchair, sometimes upset, sometimes smiling, no longer beaming. Thầy has given the world so much. He's given us, his disciples, everything. His loss is personal for us, but I realize we haven't grieved together. I think of Thầy's words: "The tears I shed yesterday have become rain." Three weeks after leaving Plum Village, my tears come. I welcome the rain that follows.

Reflection—Doing and Being

That June morning in 1992, when I lay down on my Plum Village cot, I found myself departing the world of *doing* and blissfully entering the realm of pure *being*, the ultimate dimension of interbeing. Manas, however, blocked the way, disrupting my experience of letting go by engaging its strongest *doing* allies—feeling and thinking. Fear manifesting as doubt and isolation made short shrift of my acceptance. I stood up and resumed life as a separate being.

During the more than thirty years since then, life has given me many opportunities to open my heart and keep it open for a while. To dwell in pure being for a moment, but even more important— to *do* without attachment to outcomes, without even a particular expectation, to *do* with love. To *do from a place of being*, simply being with what is. This, to me, is to be home.

Invitation

Sit in a comfortable position. Relax. Let your eyes close and breathe in and out slowly three times. Invite your life into your awareness, and notice whatever experiences, feelings, or thoughts related to the interbeing of *doing and being* come to mind. When you feel ready, open your eyes.

CONCLUSION

In some schools of Zen Buddhism students are given koans, questions to ponder that cannot be solved with reason, like "What is the sound of one hand clapping?" Students sit and live with their koan until their response conveys true insight. In the 1960s, long before I encountered Buddhism, I received a koan from a scene in the film *Breathless*, written and directed by Jean-Luc Godard. A famous philosopher who has just received a prize arrives at the Paris airport. As he steps out of the plane, a journalist asks, "What is your goal in life?" and the philosopher responds, "To become immortal and then die."

Thầy has helped me see that *death* and *immortality* are not mutually exclusive. They are the yin and yang of my life, and of this book. When I lay down on my Plum Village cot in 1992 facing death, I backed away. I'd been invited to let go, said Thầy Giác Thanh. But I wasn't ready. It's difficult for a lonely child to let go of control and trust life. Before I'd be ready, I would need to change. Life would need to change. I was to learn from Thầy that change is unnecessary, that I've been one with the cosmos from the beginning of time and always will be. The historical-dimension wave now called "Richard" will change. The water of the ultimate dimension that comprises this wave will not. Trying to become immortal as a wave is an invitation to suffer. True freedom lies in experiencing our immortality as water.

EPILOGUE

January 28, 2022

Two-and-a-half years ago on the flight home following my visit with my paralyzed Sangha friend Susan, I was overwhelmed with emotion. I tried to record the contents of my heart in my journal. But no words came until, finally, this poem:

MY TEACHER

Life enters the hall,
and I rise.
She walks slowly
to the altar,
turns, and bows.
I bow to life.
The lesson is complete.

Life was my teacher. I could say no more.

Susan passed away soon thereafter. The time that followed brought a pandemic, deeply distressing social and political events, the deaths of my brother Bob and my good friend Bill, and now Thầy. I experienced grief and many tears. Life gave me opportunities to learn profound lessons, opportunities that earlier in my life I would have buried in my unconscious or responded to with depression.

Today, Thầy was cremated in Vietnam. I thank Life for giving him to me. And I will continue to thank you, Thầy, for your teachings which have prepared me and untold others around the world to receive Life's teachings about suffering, happiness, and countless other things. Sharing my experiences with you, dear readers, is to express a small measure of my gratitude.

ACKNOWLEDGMENTS

My deepest gratitude to

Teachers and mentors who have supported my transformation and healing: Thây, Sisters Annabel and Jina, Parker Palmer, Ted Cmarada, Anh-Huong and Thu Nguyen, Rev. Paula Wehmiller, Earl Harrison, Ron McKeen, Jim Landers, and, most especially, my beloved life partner and extraordinary editor Elisabeth Dearborn. You entered my life at providential times, giving me your wisdom and your care.

Fellow teachers and spiritual friends: Irene McHenry, Kaira Jewel Lingo, Valerie Brown, John Bell, Michael Ciborski and Fern Dorresteyn, Elena Cardo, Stefano Carboni and Letizia Di Fonzo, Steve Marcus and Jesse Palidofsky. I cherish the gifts you've shared and the gifts of who you are.

Arnie Kotler, old friend and editor extraordinaire, who knew what I wanted to say and how to say it with vitality and grace; Matt Friberg, friend and editor at Parallax Press, who steered this manuscript to completion and was always available with advice and answers; Hisae Matsuda, Parallax Publisher, whose questions and feedback gave my writing direction; Katie Eberle, who took my idea for the cover and ran with it. Terry Ehling, friend and on-call editor, whose feedback led to improvements time and again; Garrett Phelan, who saw this book hidden in my unpublished memoir and insisted it be given its due; Dzung Vo, faithful early reader with perceptive feedback and enthusiasm extending to my recording an audio version; Susan Hadler, Sangha sister and writing buddy of many years, you will always be here in these pages; and my friends who have cheered me on and patiently awaited this book's release to read and review it.

THE FOURTEEN MINDFULNESS TRAININGS

The Fourteen Mindfulness Trainings are the very essence of the Order of Interbeing. They are the torch lighting our path, the boat carrying us, the teacher guiding us. They allow us to touch the nature of interbeing in everything that is, and to see that our happiness is not separate from the happiness of others. Interbeing is not a theory; it is a reality that can be directly experienced by each of us at any moment in our daily lives. The Fourteen Mindfulness Trainings help us cultivate concentration and insight which free us from fear and the illusion of a separate self.

THE FIRST MINDFULNESS TRAINING:
OPENNESS

Aware of the suffering created by fanaticism and intolerance, we are determined not to be idolatrous about or bound to any doctrine, theory, or ideology, even Buddhist ones. We are committed to seeing the Buddhist teachings as a guiding means that help us learn to look deeply and develop understanding and compassion. They are not doctrines to fight, kill, or die for. We understand that fanaticism in its many forms is the result of perceiving things in a dualistic or discriminative manner. We will train ourselves to look at everything with openness and the insight of interbeing in order to transform dogmatism and violence in ourselves and the world.

THE SECOND MINDFULNESS TRAINING:
NON-ATTACHMENT TO VIEWS

Aware of the suffering created by attachment to views and wrong perceptions, we are determined to avoid being narrow-minded and bound to present views. We are committed to learning and practicing nonattachment to views and being open to others' experiences and insights in order to benefit from the collective wisdom. We are aware that the knowledge we presently possess is not changeless, absolute truth. Insight is revealed through the practice of compassionate listening, deep looking, and letting go of notions rather than through the accumulation of intellectual knowledge. Truth is found in life, and we will observe life within and around us in every moment, ready to learn throughout our lives.

THE THIRD MINDFULNESS TRAINING:
FREEDOM OF THOUGHT

Aware of the suffering brought about when we impose our views on others, we are determined not to force others, even our children, by any means whatsoever—such as authority, threat, money, propaganda, or indoctrination—to adopt our views. We are committed to respecting the right of others to be different, to choose what to believe and how to decide. We will, however, learn to help others let go of and transform fanaticism and narrowness through loving speech and compassionate dialogue.

THE FOURTH MINDFULNESS TRAINING:
AWARENESS OF SUFFERING

Aware that looking deeply at the nature of suffering can help us develop understanding and compassion, we are determined to come home to ourselves, to recognize, accept, embrace and listen to our own suffering with the energy of mindfulness. We will do our best not to run away from our suffering or cover it up through consumption, but practice conscious breathing and walking to look deeply into the roots of our suffering. We know we can realize the path leading to the transformation of suffering only when we understand deeply the roots of suffering. Once we have understood our own suffering, we will be able to understand the suffering of others. We are committed to finding ways, including personal contact and using telephone, electronic, audiovisual, and other means, to be with those who suffer, so we can help them transform their suffering into compassion, peace, and joy.

THE FIFTH MINDFULNESS TRAINING:
COMPASSIONATE, HEALTHY LIVING

Aware that true happiness is rooted in peace, solidity, freedom, and compassion, we are determined not to accumulate wealth while millions are hungry and dying nor to take as the aim of our life fame, power, wealth, or sensual pleasure, which can bring much suffering and despair. We will practice looking deeply into how we nourish our body and mind with edible foods, sense impressions, volition, and consciousness. We are committed not to gamble or to use alcohol, drugs or any other products which bring toxins into our own and the collective body and consciousness such as certain websites, electronic games, music, TV programs, films, magazines, books and conversations. We will consume in a way that preserves compassion, well-being, and joy in our bodies and consciousness and in the collective body and consciousness of our families, our society, and the earth.

THE SIXTH MINDFULNESS TRAINING:
TAKING CARE OF ANGER

Aware that anger blocks communication and creates suffering, we are committed to taking care of the energy of anger when it arises, and to recognizing and transforming the seeds of anger that lie deep in our consciousness. When anger manifests, we are determined not to do or say anything, but to practice mindful breathing or mindful walking to acknowledge, embrace, and look deeply into our anger. We know that the roots of anger are not outside of ourselves but can be found in our wrong perceptions and lack of understanding of the suffering in ourselves and others. By contemplating impermanence, we will be able to look with the eyes of compassion at ourselves and at those we think are the cause of our anger, and to recognize the preciousness of our relationships. We will practice Right Diligence in order to nourish our capacity of understanding, love, joy and inclusiveness, gradually transforming our anger, violence and fear, and helping others do the same.

THE SEVENTH MINDFULNESS TRAINING:
DWELLING HAPPILY IN THE PRESENT MOMENT

Aware that life is available only in the present moment, we are committed to training ourselves to live deeply each moment of daily life. We will try not to lose ourselves in dispersion or be carried away by regrets about the past, worries about the future, or craving, anger, or jealousy in the present. We will practice mindful breathing to be aware of what is happening in the here and the now. We are determined to learn the art of mindful living by touching the wondrous, refreshing, and healing elements that are inside and around us, in all situations. In this way, we will be able to cultivate seeds of joy, peace, love, and understanding in ourselves, thus facilitating the work of transformation and healing in our consciousness. We are aware that real happiness depends primarily on our mental attitude and not on external conditions, and that we can live happily in the present moment simply by remembering that we already have more than enough conditions to be happy.

THE EIGHTH MINDFULNESS TRAINING:
TRUE COMMUNITY AND COMMUNICATION

Aware that lack of communication always brings separation and suffering, we are committed to training ourselves in the practice of compassionate listening and loving speech. Knowing that true community is rooted in inclusiveness and in the concrete practice of the harmony of views, thinking and speech, we will practice to share our understanding and experiences with members in our community in order to arrive at collective insight.

We are determined to learn to listen deeply without judging or reacting, and refrain from uttering words that can create discord or cause the community to break. Whenever difficulties arise, we will remain in our Sangha and practice looking deeply into ourselves and others to recognize all the causes and conditions, including our own habit energies, that have brought about the difficulties. We will take responsibility for all the ways we may have contributed to the conflict and keep communication open. We will not behave as a victim but be active in finding ways to reconcile and resolve all conflicts however small.

THE NINTH MINDFULNESS TRAINING:
TRUTHFUL AND LOVING SPEECH

Aware that words can create happiness or suffering, we are committed to learning to speak truthfully, lovingly and constructively. We will use only words that inspire joy, confidence and hope as well as promote reconciliation and peace in ourselves and among other people. We will speak and listen in a way that can help ourselves and others to transform suffering and see the way out of difficult situations. We are determined not to say untruthful things for the sake of personal interest or to impress people, nor to utter words that might cause division or hatred. We will protect the happiness and harmony of our Sangha by refraining from speaking about the faults of other persons in their absence and always ask ourselves whether our perceptions are correct. We will speak only with the intention to understand and help transform the situation. We will not spread rumors nor criticize or condemn things of which we are not sure. We will do our best to speak out about situations of injustice, even when doing so may make difficulties for us or threaten our safety.

THE TENTH MINDFULNESS TRAINING:
PROTECTING AND NOURISHING THE SANGHA

Aware that the essence and aim of a Sangha is the practice of understanding and compassion, we are determined not to use the Buddhist community for personal power or profit, or transform our community into a political instrument. As members of a spiritual community, we should nonetheless take a clear stand against oppression and injustice. We should strive to change the situation, without taking sides in a conflict. We are committed to learning to look with the eyes of interbeing and to see ourselves and others as cells in one Sangha body. As a true cell in the Sangha body, generating mindfulness, concentration, and insight to nourish ourselves and the whole community, each of us is at the same time a cell in the Buddha body. We will actively build brotherhood and sisterhood, flow as a river, and practice to develop the three real powers—understanding, love, and cutting through afflictions—to realize collective awakening.

THE ELEVENTH MINDFULNESS TRAINING:
RIGHT LIVELIHOOD

Aware that great violence and injustice have been done to our environment and society, we are committed not to live with a vocation that is harmful to humans and nature. We will do our best to select a livelihood that contributes to the well-being of all species on earth and helps realize our ideal of understanding and compassion. Aware of economic, political, and social realities around the world, as well as our interrelationship with the ecosystem, we are determined to behave responsibly as consumers and as citizens. We will not invest in or purchase from companies that contribute to the depletion of natural resources, harm the earth, or deprive others of their chance to live.

THE TWELFTH MINDFULNESS TRAINING:
REVERENCE FOR LIFE

Aware that much suffering is caused by war and conflict, we are determined to cultivate nonviolence, compassion, and the insight of interbeing in our daily lives and promote peace education, mindful mediation, and reconciliation within families, communities, ethnic and religious groups, nations, and in the world. We are committed not to kill and not to let others kill. We will not support any act of killing in the world, in our thinking, or in our way of life. We will diligently practice deep looking with our Sangha to discover better ways to protect life, prevent war, and build peace.

THE THIRTEENTH MINDFULNESS TRAINING:
GENEROSITY

Aware of the suffering caused by exploitation, social injustice, stealing, and oppression, we are committed to cultivating generosity in our way of thinking, speaking, and acting. We will practice loving kindness by working for the happiness of people, animals, plants, and minerals, and sharing our time, energy, and material resources with those who are in need. We are determined not to steal and not to possess anything that should belong to others. We will respect the property of others but will try to prevent others from profiting from human suffering or the suffering of other beings.

THE FOURTEENTH MINDFULNESS TRAINING:
TRUE LOVE

[*For lay members*]: Aware that sexual desire is not love and that sexual relations motivated by craving cannot dissipate the feeling of loneliness but will create more suffering, frustration, and isolation, we are determined not to engage in sexual relations without mutual understanding, love, and a deep long-term commitment. We resolve to find spiritual support for the integrity of our relationships from family members, friends, and sangha with whom there is support and trust. We know that to preserve the happiness of ourselves and others, we must respect the rights and commitments of ourselves and others. Recognizing the diversity of human experience, we are committed not to discriminate against any form of gender identity or sexual orientation. Seeing that body and mind are interrelated, we are committed to learning appropriate ways to take care of our sexual energy and cultivating loving kindness, compassion, joy, and inclusiveness for our own happiness and the happiness of others. We must be aware of future suffering that may be caused by sexual relations. We will treat our bodies with compassion and respect. We are determined to look deeply into the Four Nutriments and learn ways to preserve and channel our vital energies (sexual, breath, spirit) for the realization of our bodhisattva ideal. We will do everything in our power to protect children from sexual abuse and to protect couples and families from being broken by sexual misconduct. We will be fully aware of the responsibility of bringing new lives into the world and will meditate regularly upon their future environment.

[*For monastic members*]: Aware that the deep aspiration of a monk or a nun can only be realized when he or she wholly leaves behind the bonds of sensual love, we are committed to practicing chastity and to helping others protect themselves. We are aware that loneliness and suffering cannot be alleviated through a sexual relationship, but through practicing loving kindness, compassion, joy, and inclusiveness. We know that a sexual relationship will destroy our monastic life, will prevent us from realizing our ideal of serving living beings, and will harm others. We will learn appropriate ways to take care of our sexual energy. We are determined not to suppress or mistreat our body, or look upon our body as only an instrument, but will learn to handle our body with compassion and respect. We will look deeply into the Four Nutriments in order to preserve and channel our vital energies (sexual, breath, spirit) for the realization of our bodhisattva ideal.

See   *https://plumvillage.org/mindfulness/the-14-mindfulness -trainings/* for the latest version of the Fourteen Mindfulness Trainings.

THE FIVE MINDFULNESS TRAININGS

The Five Mindfulness Trainings represent the Buddhist vision for a global spirituality and ethic. They are a concrete expression of the Buddha's teachings on the Four Noble Truths and the Noble Eightfold Path, the path of right understanding and true love, leading to healing, transformation, and happiness for ourselves and for the world. To practice the Five Mindfulness Trainings is to cultivate the insight of interbeing, or Right View, which can remove all discrimination, intolerance, anger, fear, and despair. If we live according to the Five Mindfulness Trainings, we are already on the path of a bodhisattva. Knowing we are on that path, we are not lost in confusion about our life in the present or in fears about the future.

REVERENCE FOR LIFE

Aware of the suffering caused by the destruction of life, I am committed to cultivating the insight of interbeing and compassion and learning ways to protect the lives of people, animals, plants, and minerals. I am determined not to kill, not to let others kill, and not to support any act of killing in the world, in my thinking, or in my way of life. Seeing that harmful actions arise from anger, fear, greed, and intolerance, which in turn come from dualistic and discriminative thinking, I will cultivate openness, nondiscrimination, and nonattachment to views in order to transform violence, fanaticism, and dogmatism in myself and in the world.

TRUE HAPPINESS

Aware of the suffering caused by exploitation, social injustice, stealing, and oppression, I am committed to practicing generosity in my thinking, speaking, and acting. I am determined not to steal and not to possess anything that should belong to others; and I will share my time, energy, and material resources with those who are in need. I will practice looking deeply to see that the happiness and suffering of others are not separate from my own happiness and suffering; that true happiness is not possible without understanding and compassion; and that running after wealth, fame, power and sensual pleasures can bring much suffering and despair. I am aware that happiness depends on my mental attitude and not on external conditions, and that I can live happily in the present moment simply by remembering that I already have more than enough conditions to be happy. I am committed to practicing Right Livelihood so that I can help reduce the suffering of living beings on Earth and stop contributing to climate change.

TRUE LOVE

Aware of the suffering caused by sexual misconduct, I am committed to cultivating responsibility and learning ways to protect the safety and integrity of individuals, couples, families, and society. Knowing that sexual desire is not love, and that sexual activity motivated by craving always harms myself as well as others, I am determined not to engage in sexual relations without mutual consent, true love, and a deep, long-term commitment. I resolve to find spiritual support for the integrity of my relationship from family members, friends, and Sangha with whom there is support and trust. I will do everything in my power to protect children from sexual abuse and to prevent couples and families from being broken by sexual misconduct. Seeing that body and mind are interrelated, I am committed to learn appropriate ways to take care of my sexual energy and to cultivate the four basic elements of true love—loving kindness, compassion, joy, and inclusiveness—for the greater happiness of myself and others. Recognizing the diversity of human experience, I am committed not to discriminate against any form of gender identity or sexual orientation. Practicing true love, we know that we will continue beautifully into the future.

LOVING SPEECH AND DEEP LISTENING

Aware of the suffering caused by unmindful speech and the inability to listen to others, I am committed to cultivating loving speech and compassionate listening in order to relieve suffering and to promote reconciliation and peace in myself and among other people, ethnic and religious groups, and nations. Knowing that words can create happiness or suffering, I am committed to speaking truthfully using words that inspire confidence, joy, and hope. When anger is manifesting in me, I am determined not to speak. I will practice mindful breathing and walking in order to recognize and to look deeply into my anger. I know that the roots of anger can be found in my wrong perceptions and lack of understanding of the suffering in myself and in the other person. I will speak and listen in a way that can help myself and the other person to transform suffering and see the way out of difficult situations. I am determined not to spread news that I do not know to be certain and not to utter words that can cause division or discord. I will practice Right Diligence to nourish my capacity for understanding, love, joy, and inclusiveness, and gradually transform anger, violence, and fear that lie deep in my consciousness.

NOURISHMENT AND HEALING

Aware of the suffering caused by unmindful consumption, I am committed to cultivating good health, both physical and mental, for myself, my family, and my society by practicing mindful eating, drinking, and consuming. I will practice looking deeply into how I consume the Four Kinds of Nutriments, namely edible foods, sense impressions, volition, and consciousness. I am determined not to gamble, or to use alcohol, drugs, or any other products which contain toxins, such as certain websites, electronic games, TV programs, films, magazines, books, and conversations. I will practice coming back to the present moment to be in touch with the refreshing, healing and nourishing elements in me and around me, not letting regrets and sorrow drag me back into the past nor letting anxieties, fear, or craving pull me out of the present moment. I am determined not to try to cover up loneliness, anxiety, or other suffering by losing myself in consumption. I will contemplate interbeing and consume in a way that preserves peace, joy, and well-being in my body and consciousness, and in the collective body and consciousness of my family, my society and the Earth.

See *https://plumvillage.org/mindfulness/the-5-mindfulness-trainings/* for the latest version of the Five Mindfulness Trainings.

THE THREE EARTH TOUCHINGS

This is the full text guiding the practice of Three Earth Touchings that we use at our practice centers and Sanghas in the Plum Village Tradition. Practicing the Three Earth Touchings gives us an opportunity to deeply touch the reality of interbeing across space and time.

I.

Touching the Earth, I connect with ancestors and descendants of both my spiritual and my blood families.

My spiritual ancestors include the Buddha, the bodhisattvas, the noble Sangha of Buddha's disciples, [insert names of others you would like to include], and my own spiritual teachers still alive or already passed away. They are present in me because they have transmitted to me seeds of peace, wisdom, love, and happiness. They have woken up in me my resource of understanding and compassion. When I look at my spiritual ancestors, I see those who are perfect in the practice of the mindfulness trainings, understanding, and compassion, and those who are still imperfect. I accept them all because I see within myself shortcomings and weaknesses. Aware that my practice of the mindfulness trainings is not always perfect, and that I am not always as understanding and compassionate as I would like to be, I open my heart and accept all my spiritual descendants. Some of my descendants practice the mindfulness trainings, understanding, and compassion in a way which invites confidence and respect, but there are also those who come across many difficulties and are constantly subject to ups and downs in their practice.

In the same way, I accept all my ancestors on my mother's side and my father's side of the family. I accept all their good qualities and their virtuous actions, and I also accept all their weaknesses. I open my heart and accept all my blood descendants with their good qualities, their talents, and also their weaknesses.

My spiritual ancestors, blood ancestors, spiritual descendants, and blood descendants are all part of me. I am them, and they are me. I do not have a separate self. All exist as part of a wonderful stream of life which is constantly moving.

II.

Touching the Earth, I connect with all people and all species that are alive at this moment in this world with me.

I am one with the wonderful pattern of life that radiates out in all directions. I see the close connection between myself and others, how we share happiness and suffering. I am one with those who were born disabled or who have become disabled because of war, accident, or illness. I am one with those who are caught in a situation of war or oppression. I am one with those who find no happiness in family life, who have no roots and no peace of mind, who are hungry for understanding and love, and who are looking for something beautiful, wholesome, and true to embrace and to believe in. I am someone at the point of death who is very afraid and does not know what is going to happen. I am a child who lives in a place where there is miserable poverty and disease, whose legs and arms are like sticks and who has no future. I am also the manufacturer of bombs that are sold to poor countries. I am the frog swimming in the pond and I am also the snake who needs the body of the frog to nourish its own body. I am the caterpillar or the ant that the bird is looking for to eat, and I am also the bird that is looking for the caterpillar or the ant. I am the forest that is being cut down. I am the rivers and the air that are being polluted, and I am also the person who cuts down the forest and pollutes the rivers and the air. I see myself in all species, and I see all species in me.

I am one with the great beings who have realized the truth of no-birth and no-death and are able to look at the forms of birth and death, happiness and suffering, with calm eyes. I am one with those people—who can be found a little bit everywhere—who have sufficient peace of mind, understanding and love, who are able to touch what is wonderful, nourishing, and healing, who also have the capacity to embrace the world with a heart of love and arms of caring action. I am someone who has enough peace, joy, and freedom and is able to offer fearlessness and joy to living beings around themselves. I see that I am not lonely and cut off. The love and the happiness of great beings on this planet help me not to sink in despair. They help me to live my life in a meaningful way, with true peace and happiness. I see them all in me, and I see myself in all of them.

III.

Touching the Earth, I let go of my idea that I am this body and my life span is limited.

I see that this body, made up of the four elements, is not really me and I am not limited by this body. I am part of a stream of life of spiritual and blood ancestors that for thousands of years has been flowing into the present and flows on for thousands of years into the future. I am one with my ancestors. I am one with all people and all species, whether they are peaceful and fearless, or suffering and afraid. At this very moment, I am present everywhere on this planet. I am also present in the past and in the future. The disintegration of this body does not touch me, just as when the plum blossom falls it does not mean the end of the plum tree. I see myself as a wave on the surface of the ocean. My nature is the ocean water. I see myself in all the other waves and see all the other waves in me. The appearance and disappearance of the form of the wave does not affect the ocean.

My Dharma body and spiritual life are not subject to birth and death. I see the presence of myself before my body manifested and after my body has disintegrated. Even in this moment, I see how I exist elsewhere than in this body. Seventy or eighty years is not my life span. My life span, like the life span of a leaf or of a Buddha, is limitless. I have gone beyond the idea that I am a body that is separated in space and time from all other forms of life.

From   *https://plumvillage.org/key-practice-texts/the-three-earth-touchings/*

INVOKING THE
BODHISATTVAS' NAMES

We invoke your name, Avalokiteshvara. We aspire to learn your way of listening in order to help relieve the suffering in the world. You know how to listen in order to understand. We invoke your name in order to practice listening with all our attention and open-heartedness. We will sit and listen without any prejudice. We will sit and listen without judging or reacting. We will sit and listen in order to understand. We will sit and listen so attentively that we will be able to hear what the other person is saying and also what is being left unsaid. We know that just by listening deeply we already alleviate a great deal of pain and suffering in the other person.

We invoke your name, Manjushri. We aspire to learn your way, which is to be still and to look deeply into the heart of things and into the hearts of people. We will look with all our attention and open-heartedness. We will look with unprejudiced eyes. We will look without judging or reacting. We will look deeply so that we will be able to see and understand the roots of suffering and the impermanent and self-less nature of all that is. We will practice your way of using the sword of understanding to cut through the bonds of suffering, thus freeing ourselves and other species.

We invoke your name, Samantabhadra. We aspire to practice your vow to act with the eyes and heart of compassion, to bring joy to one person in the morning and to ease the pain of one person in the afternoon. We know that the happiness of others is our own happiness, and we aspire to practice joy on the path of service. We know that every word, every look, every action, and every smile can bring happiness to others. We know that if we practice wholeheartedly, we ourselves may become an inexhaustible source of peace and joy for our loved ones and for all species.

We invoke your name, Kshitigarbha. We aspire to learn your way of being present where there is darkness, suffering, oppression, and despair, so we can bring light, hope, relief, and liberation to those places. We are determined not to forget about or abandon those in desperate situations. We will do our best to establish contact with those who cannot find a way out of their suffering, those whose cries for help, justice, equality, and human rights are not being heard. We know that hell can be found in many places on Earth. We will do our best not to contribute to creating more hells on Earth, and we will help transform the hells that already exist. We will practice in order to realize the qualities of perseverance and stability, so that, like the Earth, we can always be supportive and faithful to those in need.

We invoke your name Sadaparibhuta. We aspire to learn your way of looking deeply with the eyes of non-discrimination in order to see the true qualities of others. Whenever you meet anyone, you bow respectfully and say in appreciation: "I respect you deeply. You are a future Buddha." We vow to look deeply into ourselves to recognize the positive qualities that are there, to accept and to love ourselves. We vow only to water positive seeds in ourselves and in those around us. By doing so, our thoughts, words and deeds will give rise to self-confidence and acceptance of ourselves, our children, grandchildren and all those we know. We vow to look deeply with the eyes of non-discrimination to see that the joy and success of the other person is also our joy and success. We vow to behave and to speak with humility and respect. We vow to practice loving speech to help people who underestimate themselves, see that they are wonders of the universe. We know that only when we are able to transcend the barriers of a separate self, shall we be able to transform the superiority, inferiority, and equality complexes and realize true happiness and freedom.

From *Chanting from the Heart: Buddhist Ceremonies and Daily Practices,* p. 30–32

THE FIVE REMEMBRANCES

I am of the nature to grow old. There is no way to escape growing old.

I am of the nature to have ill health. There is no way to escape ill health.

I am of the nature to die. There is no way to escape death.

All that is dear to me and everyone I love are of the nature to change. There is no way to escape being separated from them.

I inherit the results of my actions of body, speech, and mind. My actions are my continuation.

From *Chanting from the Heart: Buddhist Ceremonies and Daily Practices*, p. 51. Thich Nhat Hanh, Question and Answer Session, summer 1996.

REFERENCES

Kabir, and Robert Bly. *Kabir: Ecstatic Poems*. Boston: Beacon Press, 2004.

Boulding, Kenneth. *The Image: Knowledge in Life and Society*. Ann Arbor: University of Michigan Press, 1956.

Brady, Richard. *Walking the Teacher's Path with Mindfulness: Stories for Reflection and Action*. New York: Routledge, 2021.

Buber, Martin. *The Way of Response*. New York, Schocken Books, 1966.

Cope, Stephen. *Yoga and the Quest for the True Self*. New York: Bantam Books, 2000.

de Mille, Agnes. *Dance to the Piper & And Promenade Home: A Two-Part Autobiography*. New York: Da Capo Press, 1979.

Eliot, T. S. *Four Quartets*. Eastbourne: Gardners Books; Main edition, 2001.

Emet, Joseph, comp. *Basket of Plums Songbook: Music in the Tradition of Thich Nhat Hanh*. Berkeley: Parallax Press, 2013.

Freire, Paulo. *Pedagogy of the Oppressed*. New York: Herder and Herder, 1970.

Glasser, William. *Schools without Failure*. New York: Harper & Row, 1968.

Gorman, George. *The Amazing Fact of Quaker Worship*. London: Quaker Home Service, 1979.

Grubb, Sarah. *Some Account of the Life and Religious Labours of Sarah Grubb*. 2nd ed. London: James Phillips, 1794.

Heifetz, Ronald. *Leadership without Easy Answers*. Cambridge: Harvard University Press, 1998.

Heinlein, Robert. *Stranger in a Strange Land*. New York: Berkley Publishing Group, 1968.

Heschel, Abraham Joshua. *A Passion for Truth*. New York: Farrar, Straus and Giroux, 1973.

Kesey, Ken. *One Flew over the Cuckoo's Nest*. New York: Penguin, 1964.

Kinder, George. *The Seven Stages of Money Maturity: Understanding the Spirit and Value of Money in Your Life*. New York: Dell, 1999.

Kirshenbaum, Mira, and Charles Foster. *Parent/Teen Breakthrough: The Relationship Approach*. New York: Plume, 1991.

McCourt, Frank. *Teacher Man: A Memoir*. New York: Scribner, 2005.

McHenry, Irene, and Richard Brady. *Tuning In: Mindfulness in Teaching and Learning*. Philadelphia: Friends Council on Education, 2009.

Merton, Thomas. *The Way of Chuang Tzu*. New York: New Directions, 1965.

Miller, Henry. *Tropic of Cancer*. New York: Grove Press, 1968.

Neill, A. S. *Summerhill: A Radical Approach to Child Rearing*. New York: Hart, 1960.

Nhat Hanh, Thich. *Answers from the Heart: Practical Responses to Life's Burning Questions*. Berkeley: Parallax Press, 2009.

Nhat Hanh, Thich. *The Art of Living*. New York: HarperOne, 2017.

Nhat Hanh, Thich. *At Home in the World: Stories and Essential Teachings from a Monk's Life*. Berkeley: Parallax Press, 2016.

Nhat Hanh, Thich. *Awakening of the Heart: Essential Buddhist Sutras and Commentaries*. Berkeley: Parallax Press, 2011.

Nhat Hanh, Thich. *The Blooming of a Lotus: Guided Meditation Exercises for Healing and Transformation*. Boston: Beacon Press, 1993.

Nhat Hanh, Thich. *Breathe, You Are Alive: The Sutra on the Full Awareness of Breathing*. Berkeley: Parallax Press, 2008.

Nhat Hanh, Thich. *Calming the Fearful Mind: A Zen Response to Terrorism*. Parallax Press: Berkeley, 2001.

Nhat Hanh, Thich. *Cultivating the Mind of Love: The Practice of Looking Deeply in the Mahayana Buddhist Tradition*. Berkeley: Parallax Press, 1996.

Nhat Hanh, Thich. *Friends on the Path: Living in Spiritual Communities*. Berkeley: Parallax Press, 2002.

Nhat Hanh, Thich. *The Heart of the Buddha's Teachings: Transforming Suffering into Peace, Joy, and Liberation*. New York: Broadway Books, 1999.

Nhat Hanh, Thich. *The Heart of Understanding: Commentaries on the Prajnaparamita Heart Sutra*. Berkeley: Parallax Press, 1988.

Nhat Hanh, Thich. *How to Love*. Berkeley: Parallax Press, 2015.

Nhat Hanh, Thich. *Inside the Now: Meditations on Time*. Berkeley: Parallax Press, 2015.

Nhat Hanh, Thich. *Interbeing: The 14 Mindfulness Trainings of Engaged Buddhism*. 4th ed. Berkeley: Parallax Press, 2020.

Nhat Hanh, Thich. *Living Buddha, Living Christ.* New York: Riverhead Books, 1995.

Nhat Hanh, Thich. *The Miracle of Mindfulness: A Manual on Meditation.* Boston: Beacon Press, 1975.

Nhat Hanh, Thich. *No Mud, No Lotus: The Art of Transforming Suffering.* Berkeley: Parallax Press, 2014.

Nhat Hanh, Thich. *Old Path, White Clouds: Walking in the Footsteps of the Buddha.* Berkeley: Parallax Press, 1987.

Nhat Hanh, Thich. *The Path of Emancipation.* Berkeley: Parallax Press, 2000.

Nhat Hanh, Thich. *Peace Is Every Step: The Path of Mindfulness in Everyday Life.* New York: Random House, 1992.

Nhat Hanh, Thich. "Please Call Me by My True Names" in *Being Peace.* Berkeley: Parallax Press, 1987.

Nhat Hanh, Thich. *Present Moment Wonderful Moment: Mindfulness Verses for Daily Living.* Berkeley: Parallax Press, 2022.

Nhat Hanh, Thich. *The Sun My Heart: From Mindfulness to Insight Contemplation.* Berkeley: Parallax Press, 1988.

Nhat Hanh, Thich. *Touching Peace: Practicing the Art of Mindful Living.* Berkeley: Parallax Press, 1992.

Nhat Hanh, Thich. *Transformation and Healing: Sutra on the Four Establishments of Mindfulness.* Berkeley: Parallax Press, 2002.

Nhat Hanh, Thich. *Transformation at the Base: Fifty Verses on the Nature of Consciousness.* Berkeley: Parallax Press, 2001.

Nhat Hanh, Thich. *Under the Rose Apple Tree.* Berkeley: Parallax Press, 2001.

Nhat Hanh, Thich. *Zen Keys: A Guide to Zen Practice.* New York: Harmony Books, 1994.

Nhat Hanh, Thich, and Katherine Weare. *Happy Teachers Change the World.* Berkeley: Parallax Press, 2017.

Nhat Hanh, Thich, and the Monks and Nuns of Plum Village. *Chanting from the Heart: Buddhist Ceremonies and Daily Practices.* Berkeley: Parallax Press, 2007.

Palmer, Parker. *To Know As We Are Known: A Spirituality of Education.* San Francisco: Harper & Row, 1983.

Postman, Neil, and Charles Weingartner. *Teaching As a Subversive Activity.* New York: Delta, 1969.

Thurman, Howard. *The Living Wisdom of Howard Thurman: A Visionary for Our Time.* Colorado: Sounds True, 2010. Audio CD.

Weiss, Andrew. *Beginning Mindfulness: Learning the Way of Awareness, A Ten-Week Course.* Novato, CA: New World Library, 2004.

Whitman, Walt. *Leaves of Grass.* New York: The Modern Library, 1993.

Wolfe, Thomas. *Look Homeward Angel: A Story of the Buried Life.* New York: Simon & Schuster, 1995.

SELECTED RESOURCES

Other books I've found important:

Bell, John. *Unbroken Wholeness: Six Pathways to Beloved Community.* Berkeley: Parallax Press, 2024.

Brown, Valerie, Marisela B. Gomez, MD, and Kaira Jewel Lingo. *Healing Our Way Home.* Berkeley: Parallax Press, 2024.

Chödrön, Pema. *When Things Fall Apart: Heart Advice for Difficult Times.* Boston: Shambhala Publications, 1996.

Dass, Ram. *Be Here Now.* San Cristobal, NM: Lama Foundation, 1971.

de Saint-Exupéry, Antoine. *The Little Prince.* Trans. by Richard Howard. New York: Clarion Books, 2000.

Giono, Jean. *The Man Who Planted Trees.* 20th ed. Chelsea Green, 2007.

Greenleaf, Robert K. *The Servant As Leader.* Rev. ed. Westfield, IN: Greenleaf Center for Servant Leadership, 2008.

Housden, Roger, ed. *Risking Everything: 110 Poems of Love and Revelation.* New York: Harmony Books, 2003.

Kushner, Lawrence. *Invisible Lines of Connection: Sacred Stories of the Ordinary.* Woodstock, VT: Jewish Lights, 1996.

Lama, Dalai, Desmond Tutu, and Douglas Abrams. *The Book of Joy: Lasting Happiness in a Changing World.* New York: Avery, 2016.

Leaf, Munro. *The Story of Ferdinand.* New York: Grosset & Dunlap, 2011.

Lingo, Kaira Jewel. *We Were Made for These Times: 10 Lessons for Moving Through Change, Loss, and Disruption.* Berkeley: Parallax Press, 2021.

Nhat Hanh, Thich. *Being Peace.* Berkeley: Parallax Press, 1987.

Nhat Hanh, Thich. *Fear: Essential Wisdom for Getting Through the Storm.* New York: HarperOne, 2014.

Nhat Hanh, Thich. *Happiness: Essential Mindfulness Practices.* Berkeley: Parallax Press, 2009.

Nhat Hanh, Thich. *How to Relax*. Berkeley: Parallax Press, 2015.

Nhat Hanh, Thich. *The Pocket Thich Nhat Hanh*. Ed. by Melvin McLeod. Boston: Shambhala Publications, 2012.

Nhat Hanh, Thich. *You Are Here: Discovering the Magic of the Present Moment*. Boston: Shambhala Publications, 2010.

Nhat Hanh, Thich, and Chan Khong. *Zen and the Art of Saving the Planet*. Ed. by Sister True Dedication. New York: HarperOne, 2021.

Ostaseski, Frank, and Rachel Naomi Remen. *The Five Invitations: Discovering What Death Can Teach Us About Living Fully*. New York: Flatiron Books, 2019.

Palmer, Parker. *The Courage to Teach: Exploring the Inner Landscape of a Teacher's Life*. San Francisco: Jossey-Bass, 1998.

Parnes, Sidney J. *The Magic of Your Mind*. Buffalo, NY: Creative Education Foundation, 1981.

Remen, Rachel Naomi. *Kitchen Table Wisdom: Stories that Heal*. New York: Riverhead Books, 1997.

Remen, Rachel Naomi. *My Grandfather's Blessings: Stories of Strength, Refuge, and Belonging*. New York: Riverhead Books, 2000.

Rinpoche, Yongey Mingyur. *The Joy of Living: Unlocking the Secret and Science of Happiness*. New York: Three Rivers Press, 2007.

Rosen, Jo-ann. *Unshakeable: Trauma-Informed Mindfulness for Collective Awakening*. Berkeley: Parallax Press, 2023.

Rosenberg, Marshall. *Nonviolent Communication: A Language of Life*. 3rd ed. . Encinitas, CA: PuddleDancer Press, 2015.

Suzuki, Shunryu. *Zen Mind, Beginner's Mind*. New York: Weatherhill, 1970.

Varley, Susan. *Badger's Parting Gifts*. New York: HarperCollins, 1984.

Zander, Rosamund Stone, and Benjamin Zander. *The Art of Possibility: Transforming Professional and Personal Life*. London: Penguin, 2002.

COMMUNITY RESOURCES

The Plum Village App a free app with guided meditations, deep relaxations and other practices offered by Zen master Thich Nhat Hanh and his monastic community *https://plumvillage.app/*

The Way Out Is In podcast series aimed at helping transcend fear and anger to enable more engagement in the world in a way that develops love and compassion *https://plumvillage.org/podcasts/the-way-out-is-in*

Websites

ARISE Sangha: Awakening through Race, Intersectionality, and Social Equity engaging the global community in the work of healing through social action *www.arisesangha.org*

Earth Holder Community a mindful earth justice initiative in the Plum Village Community of Engaged Buddhism *www.earthholder.training*

Happy Farms actively promoting mindfulness, community-building and sustainability *www.thehappyfarm.org*

Parallax Press publisher of more than a hundred books by Thich Nhat Hanh and also the publishing home of authors writing on mindfulness in daily life; contemplative practice; personal and collective healing; and activism for peace, the protection of the Earth, and social justice *https://www.parallax.org/*

The Mindfulness Bell a journal of the art of mindful living, published three times a year by Plum Village—an inspiration and teaching resource for those practicing mindfulness in daily life *https://www.parallax.org/mindfulnessbell/*

Thich Nhat Hanh Foundation working to continue the teachings and practice of Thich Nhat Hanh *https://thichnhathanhfoundation.org/*

Wake Up Network an active global community of young mindfulness practitioners, aged 18–35, inspired by the teachings of Zen Master and peace activist Thich Nhat Hanh *https://plumvillage.org/community/wake-up-young-practitioners*

Wake Up Schools a Plum Village initiative to bring the practices of mindfulness and applied ethics into educators' own lives so they may be happy and free, and so they may in turn share these practices with colleagues and students in their school communities *https://wakeupschools.org/*

NOTES

1 Diagram from *https://plumvillage.app/our-mind-and-mental-formations/*. For a very thorough discussion of the Buddha's teachings on the nature of consciousness, see Nhat Hanh, *Transformation at the Base*.

2 Richard Brady, *Walking the Teacher's Path with Mindfulness: Stories for Reflection and Action* (New York: Routledge, 2021).

3 Thich Nhat Hanh, *The Heart of the Buddha's Teaching: Transforming Suffering into Peace, Joy, and Liberation* (New York: Broadway Books, 1999), p. 100.

4 For more information, see *The Heart of the Buddha's Teaching*, pp. 31–7.

5 Sarah Grubb, *Some Account of the Life and Religious Labours of Sarah Grubb*, 2nd Edition. London: James Phillips, 1794), p. 198.

6 For more information on the Myers-Briggs Type Indicator see: Wikipedia, "Myers-Briggs Type Indicator," accessed October 10, 2020, *https://en. wikipedia.org/wiki/Myers%E2%80%93Briggs_Type_Indicator*.

7 Traditionally, in Buddhism, the fourfold Sangha consists of monks, nuns, laymen, and laywomen who support and practice the Dharma, the teachings of the Buddha. Thich Nhat Hanh sometimes used the term Sangha in the traditional way, but as often as not he referred to Sangha as the community that supports the spiritual practice of its members, which includes not only people, but birds, whose calls invite mindful attention, and stars that announce their presence in the sky. Family members are vital members of my non-Buddhist Sangha, constantly offering me opportunities to deepen my practice.

8 For the most recent issue, past issues, and subscriptions, see https://www.parallax.org/mindfulnessbell/.

9 For the current International Sangha Directory, see *https://plumvillage .org/community/international-sangha-directory*.

10 In the late 1990s *Dharma discussion* was renamed *Dharma sharing* because it involves sharing but not discussion.

11 Based on the description of Dharma sharing at https://plumvillage.org/.

12 Thomas Merton, *The Way of Chuang Tzu* (New York: New Directions, 1965), pp. 110–11.

13 Thich Nhat Hanh, *The Miracle of Mindfulness: A Manual on Meditation* (Boston: Beacon Press, 1975), pp. 5–6.

14 From https://www.floridamindfulness.org/Refuge.

15 Also see Thich Nhat Hanh, *The Blooming of a Lotus: Guided Meditation Exercises for Healing and Transformation* (Boston: Beacon Press, 1993), p. 21.

16 In 1982 Thich Nhat Hanh purchased two parcels of land of eighty acres in total in the rural Dordogne department of Southwestern France. The first became Lower Hamlet, a residence for nuns and laywomen. Upper Hamlet, about two miles away, would become home for monks and laymen. Their two-hundred-year-old stone houses and buildings which originally housed sheep, pigs, and cattle were converted into dormitories, kitchens, offices, and small meditation halls.

17 Thich Nhat Hanh and the Monks and Nuns of Plum Village, *Chanting from the Heart: Buddhist Ceremonies and Daily Practices* (Berkeley: Parallax Press, 2007), p. 51.

18 For the Diamond Sutra, see Thich Nhat Hanh, *Cultivating the Mind of Love: The Practice of Looking Deeply in the Mahayana Buddhist Tradition* (Berkeley: Parallax Press, 1996), ch. 7.

19 For the Lotus Sutra, see Nhat Hanh, *Cultivating the Mind of Love*, ch. 14

20 For the Avatamsaka Sutra, see Nhat Hanh, *Cultivating the Mind of Love*, ch. 13.

21 Retreats in most Buddhist traditions focus on silent formal practice. By contrast, the Plum Village tradition focuses on mindfulness around the clock; formal silent practice is part of this wider focus on mindfulness.

22 Thich Nhat Hanh, *Under the Rose Apple Tree* (Berkeley: Parallax Press, 2001), p. 9.

23 Thich Nhat Hanh, Question and Answer Session, summer 1996.

24 Nhat Hanh et al. *Chanting from the Heart*, pp. 249–250.

25 Sojun Mel Weitsman in "The Problems You Are Experiencing Now … " (Berkeley Zen Center, DHARMA, August 29, 2016), *https://berkeley zencenter.org/category/dharma/page/4/*.

26 *https://plumvillage.org/mindfulness/extended-practises/#beginning-anew*, 2023).

27 Thich Nhat Hanh, Present Moment Wonderful Moment: Mindfulness Verses for Daily Living (Berkeley: Parallax Press, 2022), p. 3.

28 Nhat Hanh et al., *Chanting from the Heart*, p. 285.

29 Many of these songs can be found in the *Basket of Plums Songbook*.

30 https://www.youtube.com/watch?v=OEsMlW3mB4I

31 Nhat Hanh et al., *Chanting from the Heart*, pp. 30–32.

32 Howard Thurman, *The Living Wisdom of Howard Thurman: A Visionary for Our Time*. Colorado: Sounds True, 2010, audio CD.

33 See Nhat Hanh, *The Blooming of a Lotus*, p. 21.

34 Richard Brady and Audrey Russek. "The Reward Is Tremendous" in *The Mindfulness Bell*, No. 15, Winter 1995–96.

35 Thich Nhat Hanh, *Touching Peace: Practicing the Art of Mindful Living* (Berkeley: Parallax Press, 1992), pp. 11–12.

36 For conference videos and materials, other resources, and to sign up on the MiEN listserv, visit: http://www.mindfuled.org/.

37 See *https://www.woodyguthrie.org/Lyrics/This_Land.htm*.

38 Agnes de Mille, *Dance to the Piper & And Promenade Home: A Two-Part Autobiography* (New York: Da Capo Press, 1979) p. 335.

39 Richard Brady, "Realizing True Education with *Mindfulness*" (*available here: https://www.mindingourlives.net/resources/#articles*).

40 See *https://plumvillage.app/listening-to-namo-avalokiteshvara/*.

41 Thich Nhat Hanh, "The Next Buddha May Be a Sangha" in *Inquiring Mind*, Vol 10, No. 2, Spring 1994.

42 Thầy's 2008 retreat at The Doon School in Dehradun for Indian educators was an early expression of the Applied Ethics initiative that manifested in the EIAB retreat of 2011. This Plum Village education initiative was renamed "Wake Up Schools" in 2013. Extensive information, resources, and subscription for the Wake Up Schools newsletter are available at https://wakeupschools.org/.

43 Sharing intentions at the beginning of a workshop can give leaders a sense of participant expectations. While this can help leaders fine-tune their teaching, it reinforces the role of participants as individual receivers. When all, including the teacher, share gifts they've brought with them to a retreat, the community begins to discover the assets all may draw on. This helps a feeling of Sangha begin to manifest. Gifts shared in retreats I've led have included: listening, humor, compassion, tears, and song.

44   Irving Berlin's "Blue Skies" sung by Frank Sinatra *https://www.google
.com/search?tbm=vid&sxsrf=AJOqlzXwEcqiJkBFOIzXwgSZqJeRehan
3A:1677901212771&q=blue+skies+frank+sinatra+tommy+dorsey&sa
=X&ved=2ahUKEwiwi4WOrcH9AhWcEVkFHdCMCZcQ8ccDegQIDB
AH&biw=1280&bih=613&dpr=1.5#fpstate=ive&vld=cid:3a7adaba,vid
:h03eH51rsuM.*

45   Thich Nhat Hanh, "Please Call Me by My True Names" in *Being Peace*
(Berkeley: Parallax Press, 1987), pp. 63–64.

46   See Chapters 13 and 14 for my account of moving to Vermont in 2008
and beginning to write "Vermont Reflections."

47   Kenneth Boulding, *The Image: Knowledge in Life and Society* (Ann
Arbor: University of Michigan Press, 1956).

48   Ronald Heifetz, *Leadership without Easy Answers* (Cambridge: Harvard
University Press, 1998).

49   Kabir and Robert Bly, *Kabir: Ecstatic Poems* (Boston: Beacon Press,
2004), p. 45.

50   See Thich Nhat Hanh, *Transformation and Healing: Sutra on the Four
Establishments of Mindfulness* (Berkeley: Parallax Press, 2002).

51   William Glasser, *Schools without Failure* (New York: Harper & Row,
1968).

52   Kirshenbaum, Mira, and Charles Foster. *Parent/Teen Breakthrough: The
Relationship Approach* (New York: Plume, 1991), p. 143.

53   Thich Nhat Hanh, *Breathe, You Are Alive: The Sutra on the Full Awareness
of Breathing* (Berkeley: Parallax Press, 2008).

54   "No Coming, No Going" on *Journey to Nowhere* recorded by Blue Cliff
Ensemble featuring Nigel Armstrong (Plum Village Records, 2017),
available here: *https://www.youtube.com/watch?v=uzLtrtDyO0k*.

55   Thomas Wolfe, *Look Homeward Angel: A Story of the Buried Life* (New
York: Simon & Schuster, 1995), p. 1.

56   Walt Whitman, *Leaves of Grass* (New York: The Modern Library, 1993),
p. 113.

57   Thầy's teachings from this retreat appear in his book *The Art of Living*
(New York: HarperOne, 2017).

PERMISSIONS

ABOUT THE AUTHOR

Richard Brady is a writer, retreat leader, and consultant for mindfulness in education. He taught high school mathematics in Washington, DC for thirty-seven years. In 1989, he co-founded the Washington Mindfulness Community, a practice community in the Plum Village tradition. In 1992, he joined Thich Nhat Hanh's Order of Interbeing where he was given the Dharma name True Dharma Bridge, and in 2001 Thich Nhat Hanh ordained him as a Dharma teacher in the Plum Village Tradition with a focus on cultivating mindfulness in young people.

That same year, Richard founded the Mindfulness in Education Network to support mindfulness in educational settings. He is the North American coordinator of the Plum Village Wake Up Schools program which supports educators using and sharing mindfulness practice in their school environments. He also coordinates Wake Up Schools' Happy Teacher Sangha of the Americas which nurtures self-care and offers monthly space for teachers to practice and connect with one another.

A longtime mindfulness practitioner, Richard has led many mindfulness retreats for educators in the US and Europe. He is the author of *Walking the Teacher's Path with Mindfulness: Stories for Reflection and Action* and coeditor of *Tuning In: Mindfulness in Teaching and Learning*. For more about Richard and his writings, visit mindingourlives.net and shortjourneyhome.com.

Monastics and visitors practice the art of mindful living in the tradition of Thich Nhat Hanh at our mindfulness practice centers around the world. To reach any of these communities, or for information about how individuals, couples, and families can join in a retreat, please contact:

PLUM VILLAGE
33580 Dieulivol, France
plumvillage.org

LA MAISON DE L'INSPIR
77510 Villeneuve-sur-Bellot, France
maisondelinspir.org

HEALING SPRING
MONASTERY
77510 Verdelot, France
healingspringmonastery.org

MAGNOLIA GROVE
MONASTERY
Batesville, MS 38606, USA
magnoliagrovemonastery.org

BLUE CLIFF MONASTERY
Pine Bush, NY 12566, USA
bluecliffmonastery.org

DEER PARK MONASTERY
Escondido, CA 92026, USA
deerparkmonastery.org

EUROPEAN INSTITUTE OF
APPLIED BUDDHISM
D-51545 Waldbröl, Germany
eiab.eu

THAILAND PLUM VILLAGE
Nakhon Ratchasima
30130 Thailand
thaiplumvillage.org

ASIAN INSTITUTE OF
APPLIED BUDDHISM
Lantau Island, Hong Kong
pvfhk.org

STREAM ENTERING
MONASTERY
Beaufort, Victoria 3373
Australia
nhapluu.org

MOUNTAIN SPRING
MONASTERY
Bilpin, NSW 2758, Australia
mountainspringmonastery.org

For more information visit: *plumvillage.org*
To find an online sangha visit: *plumline.org*
For more resources, try the Plum Village app: *plumvillage.app*
Social media: *@thichnhathanh @plumvillagefrance*

PARALLAX PRESS, a nonprofit publisher founded by Zen Master Thich Nhat Hanh, publishes books and media on the art of mindful living and Engaged Buddhism. We are committed to offering teachings that help transform suffering and injustice. Our aspiration is to contribute to collective insight and awakening, bringing about a more joyful, healthy, and compassionate society.

View our entire library at parallax.org.

THE MINDFULNESS BELL is a journal of the art of mindful living in the Plum Village tradition of Thich Nhat Hanh. To subscribe or to see the worldwide directory of Sanghas (local mindfulness groups), visit mindfulnessbell.org.